Praise for Angela Spenc ~

A Taste of Florida and the Keys

"You're in for a treat when you purchase this organized cookbook. The recipes are not only reliable, but delicious. The Best Conch Fritters with Mango-Mustard Sauce, Coconut Shrimp and Chocolate Key Lime Pie were my favorites."
—Richard Clementine, San Diego, CA

"I am a native Floridian and was totally surprised at how accurate the history and recipes were."
—Kathleen Turner, Key West

"This cookbook covers it all—everything from conch fritters and authentic Key Lime Pie Recipes. Some are original Latin recipes, others are Caribbean and Southern-based dishes."
—Sophie Jordan, Orlando

"Even if you can't or don't like cooking, this is the book you need. Numbered, easy-to-follow instructions, readily found ingredients, and above all, entertaining tidbits and Florida and cooking in general."
—Paul Scarsdale, St. Augustine

A Taste of the Caribbean

"I bought this book for its cover. I have cooked my way through nearly the entire book, and admit to having stolen some of the recipes and adapted them. The recipes are good, and the information accurate."
—Esther Mathews, St. Croix, U.S. Virgin Islands

"I am a native Virgin Islander and recommend this book to anyone interested in Caribbean cooking. Some of the recipes are just like the ones my grandmother used to make."
—Lorna P. Brathwaite, St. Thomas, U.S. Virgin Islands

Just Add Rum!

"Want to throw a Caribbean party? Don't want to spend days preparing? Here's the answer to your prayers, Just Add Rum! No problem, mon."
— GEORGE L., SARASOTA, FL

"I can trust Angela Spenceley to give me a recipe that works with a manageable amount of ingredients. The rum desserts in this cookbook are just to-die-for. I made the Fallen Chocolate Rum Cake for my sister's rehearsal dinner. The guests couldn't stop raving about it."
— LUCINDA J., MIAMI, FLORIDA

A Taste of Puerto Rico, Too!

"This book is awesome. Having tried several of the authentic Puerto Rican recipes, Arroz Con Pollo, Chicken Asopao, Roast Pork with Aji-li-Mojili Sauce, I drooled over trying the rest. I like that substitutions were listed for some of the more exotic ingredients."
— MARIA ALVAREZ, NEW YORK

"I was born in Ponce, Puerto Rico, but moved to Chicago when I was four. I've been looking for a good Puerto Rican cookbook for a long time. A Taste of Puerto Rico, Too! answered my prayers. Now my husband comes home to a real Puerto Rican dinner every night. Thank you so much."
— GLADYS MODANADO, CHICAGO

"Terrific recipes, simple to make. I liked all the cooking hints and comments made with each recipe."
— THOMAS BRANCH, PEMBROKE, MA

A Taste of FLORIDA and the KEYS

ALSO BY ANGELA SPENCELEY

A Taste of FLORIDA and the KEYS

Angela Spenceley

COVER ILLUSTRATION
Giovanne Mitchell

Coconut Press
St. Thomas, U.S. Virgin Islands

A Taste of Florida, The Keys and Caribbean

Printed in India

Distributed by:

Coconut Press, Inc.
P.O. Box 309540
St. Thomas, U.S. Virgin Islands 00803
writer@islands.vi

For additional copies or bulk sales, contact Coconut Press.
www.coconut-press.com

First Edition Published 2007

UPC 704441 52121 5
ISBN 10: 0-9778913-1-3
ISBN 13: 978-0-9778913-1-3
EAN 978-097789131 3
EAN 5 51499

Library of Congress Control Number: 2001012345

Book Design by Dotti Albertine

CONTENTS

🌴 A Taste of Florida

Introduction to Florida and Culinary History

PREHISTORIC Florida's first settler's were not explorers or adventurers, but hunters and gatherers whose diet consisted mostly of small animals, plants, nuts, seeds and seafood. Occasionally these nomads tracked big game animals for food. Prehistoric animals included the mammals we are familiar with today, horses, bison and camels, along with the now extinct mastodon, giant armadillo, and saber-tooth tiger.

Twelve thousand years ago, the Florida coastline was much different from today. For starters, the sea level was lower, rendering the Florida peninsula more than twice as big as it is now. Despite less plentiful rainfall, Florida's wide variety of climates supports an abundance of plant and animal life.

During the period prior to the arrival of the Europeans, the first Floridians, settled in areas of plentiful water, stones for tool manufacture, and firewood. As the population increased, tribes moved inland where they could grow corn, beans, squash and other foodstuffs.

Over the centuries, complex cultures developed, along with cultivated agriculture and trade with other groups. Some tribes buried their dead in elaborate ceremonies, decorating with elaborate pottery in earthen mounds.

The first written record about Florida began in 1513 with the arrival of Ponce de Leon on the northeast coast, perhaps near what is now known as St. Augustine. He called the area la Florida, in honor of Pascua florida (feast of flowers) Spain's spring celebration.

On his second voyage in 1521, Ponce de Leon landed on the southwestern coast of the peninsula. Intending to start a colony, he came with 250 men, 50 horses and other farm animals and equipment. His attempts at colonization quickly failed when the native people began attacking. Ponce de Leon was wounded by an Indian arrow and died several weeks later in Havana.

Hernando de Soto's expedition, in search of gold and silver, passed through Florida in 1539, bringing additional farm animals, which initiated a diet change in an area solely dependant upon small game and fish. In 1558 Tristan de Luna y Arellano established a small and short lived, colony in Pensacola.

In the meantime, trade lines developed, and the Spanish shipped vessels heavily laden with gold, silver, and other luxuries, through the Gulf Stream and the straits that paralleled Florida's Keys. This shipping route was called the Spanish Main. Pirates preyed. Pirates preyed on these fleets, and hurricanes created additional hazards, resulting in numerous shipwrecks along the coast.

In 1562, the French protestant Jean Ribault lead an expedition to Florida, and 2 years later Rene Goulaine de Laudonniere founded Fort Caroline at the mouth of the St. Johns river, near what is today Jacksonville.

France's subsequent interest in Florida accelerated Spain's colonization plans. Pedro Menendez de Aviles founded St. Augustine in 1565 as the first permanent European city in the current area of the United States. He ousted or killed the French and others that did not believe in the Roman Catholic church. This began the Spanish tradition of building Catholic missions throughout the Southeastern United States. Menendez later attacked Fort Caroline, killing all the French soldiers, and renamed the settlement San Mateo.

It was this founding of St. Augustine, and the subsequent Nombre de Dios missions that brought European cuisine to Florida. Franciscan friars traveling to Pensacola produced delectable eggs custards from Spain. The use of rice and spices was also introduced at this time.

Much of what changed the face of Spanish cooking were the Moors and Africans that came at first as free people with the Conquistadors, then the thousands that came as slaves in the middle of the 6teenth century.

The French paid back the Spanish for the massacre at Fort Caroline when Dominique de Gourgues recaptured San Mateo and executed all the Spanish soldiers. In 1586, part-time pirate and part-time sea captain, Sir Francis Drake, plundered and burned St. Augustine. The Africans brought with them yams, eggplants, okra and sesame seeds, incorporating this into Spanish cuisine.

English settler's who arrived in 1600 were well aware of Spain's control over southeastern United States, and settled up North—at Jamestown in 1607 and Plymouth in 1620. The English gradually pushed Spanish territory south, while the French along the Mississippi River encroached from the west. In 1702, English Colonel James Moore and his allies attacked and destroyed St. Augustine, but not the fort. Within two years they destroyed many Spanish missions between Tallahassee and St. Augustine, executing any Indians friendly with the Spaniards. Later in 1719, the French captured Pensacola.

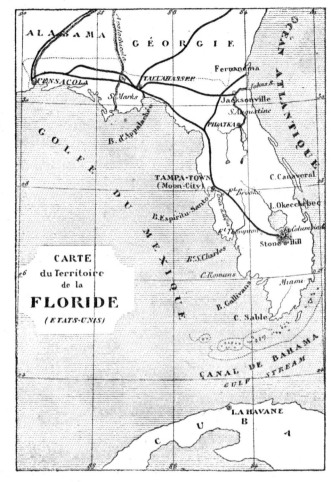

Spain's foothold weakened more when England founded Georgia in 1733, who in turn attacked the fort at St. Augustine unsuccessfully for over a month.

Thirty years later, Spain traded Florida to Britain in exchange for Havana, Cuba, formerly acquired by the British from Spain during the Seven Year's War (1756-63). Nearly all the Spanish inhabitants, along with the natives, left Florida.

The British divided the peninsula into East Florida with its capital at St. Augustine and West Florida—Pensacola. Needing settlers the Brits began giving away free land and money for businesses. Around this time, Creek Indians migrated into Florida forming the Seminole tribe.

During the American Revolutionary War, Spain, allied with France now, recaptured parts of West Florida. In 1784, the Treaty of Paris ended the war, returning all of Florida to Spain. Unfortunately, no boundaries were specified. In the Treaty of San Lorenzo of 1795, Spain recognized the 31st parallel as the boundary of Florida.

The British departed Florida, and former Spanish colonists and other settlers returned lured by lucrative free land deals. These northern settlers brought their own brand of cuisines—sweets, quick hot breads, and rice cooked differently from the Spanish. It wasn't until after the civil war, when the Spanish migrated to Key West and Tampa, that European-style wheat breads came into vogue. Interestingly, Pensacola came up with a type of hardtack made for a salad called gaspachee.

After the Revolutionary War, Key West was settled by refugees from the war, many Brits and Bahamians. The English introduced steamed puddings, rice and peas seasoned with hot peppers and the infamous 'Key Lime Pie', made from local Key limes and canned condensed milk.

Black and white settler's from Southern colonies established a new type of gastro-nomic delight—soul food or Cracker cooking. The British influence over Spanish-Cracker cooking never allowed it to reach the fiery, spicy heights of Spanish California cuisines.

In 1768, a group of Minorcans (people from Italy, Greece and the island of Minorca) came over as indentured servants and brought their own style of cooking, which featured a fiery pepper known as the Datil. They also blessed Florida with their delectable coconut treats and cheese pastries.

After several military operations led by the United States, Spain ceded Florida to the U.S. in 1821 with the signing of the Adams-Onis Treaty. During one of these military events, General Andrew Jackson led the First Seminole War in 1818.

The territory of Florida became an organized territory of the U.S. in 1822, merging East and West Florida. As more people settled in Florida, the United States government was pressured to remove the Indians, who often harbored runaway slaves. Truth was the settlers wanted Indian lands.

In 1832, the U.S. signed the Treaty of Pyane's Landing with some of the Seminole Indian chiefs. If the Indians voluntarily left Florida, they would receive land west of the Mississippi River in Oklahoma. The remaining Seminoles prepared for war. In 1835, the Second Seminole War, which lasted until 1842. cost the U.S. government some $20,000.00. Eventually some Indians migrated voluntarily, others escaped into the

Everglades. Today gambling casinos can be seen on the reservations at Big Cypress Swamp, near Okeechobee, Immokalee and Hollywood.

By the time Florida became the 27th state on March 3, 1845, the population reached some 54,000 people, half of which were African American slaves.

With Abraham Lincoln's election in 1860, Florida, as well as other slave states, seceded from the Union on January 10, 1861 to become the Confederate States of America. It wasn't until around the Civil War that small groups of Jews came to Florida to seek out livelihoods as farmers, merchants and planters—Florida being a main supply route for the Confederate Army. The recently arrived Jewish settlers adapted locally available food to their dietary laws. Later in the early twentieth century, the real estate boom brought numerous Jewish investors, and Jewish restaurants appeared all over Miami.

Florida wasn't as badly devastated as several other Southern states by the civil war. However, life did change. Jacksonville and Pensacola, both sea ports, fared well because of the demand for lumber to rebuild. Slaves were freed, and plantation owners unsuccessfully tried to hire former slaves to pick cotton. On July 25, 1868, Florida was readmitted to the United States.

During the latter nineteenth century, railroads opened routes to South and Central Florida, and gave way to luxury hotels. Henry Plant, a railroad magnate, built a fabulous hotel in Tampa, which is now the campus for the University of Tampa. Henry Flagler, a name you will see mentioned all over Florida, constructed the railroad from Jacksonville to Key West, as well as luxury hotels. All of this railway construction influenced Florida cuisines again. Northern wives, instead of baking apple pie, created mango tarts, and likewise from the luscious tropical fare: guava, citrus, and fresh seafood. At this time, large-scale commercial development, i.e. cattle-raising, and cigar manufacturing took place.

Other investors initiated such ventures as sponge harvesting in Tarpon Springs, also the best-known first Greek Community in Florida. Hence, Greek food and olive oil was introduced to the peninsula. The citrus industry took off like wild-wire, and other rapidly growing industries prompted the construction of even more railways. As early as the 1870's northern tourists visited Florida for its semi-tropical climate, swaying palms, and white sand beaches.

In 1898, Florida became the staging area for U.S. troops headed for Cuba in the Spanish-American War. By the turn of the century, Florida flourished from the increased population and development. After World War I, land developers flocked to the Sunshine State. Many of the winter snowbirds stayed on. The Florida Land Boom was such that even the swamps were drained to provide housing. Real estate prices reached artificially inflated highs.

What goes up usually comes down hard. And this is exactly what happened in 1926, when creditors lost trust in *investors*. Hurricanes in 1926 and 1928 further hurt the economy. In 1929, the Great Depression hit the rest of the United States, and the Mediterranean fruit fly further devastated Florida's economy, when it hit the citrus orchards, cutting their production by sixty percent.

World War II turned things around for Florida with its influx of soldiers and other military personal. New highways and airports were built to support this military infra-structure. By the end of the war, the state had an excellent transportation network to welcome new residents and visitors. Food history-wise, serviceman brought their fami-lies, who incorporated the rich tropical fare of avocados, carambolas, guavas and other exotics into their diets.

Theme parks appeared in the 1930's, which included Cypress Gardens and Marineland, and drew even more visitors. In 1959, Cuban refugees and Haitians landed in Florida, bringing their own unique cooking styles. Cuban and Haitian restaurants exploded on the Florida scene, featuring arroz con pollo, Cuban sandwiches and rice and beans.

As Florida's economy becomes more diverse due to tourism, major theme parks, cat-tle, citrus, and phosphate, the population constantly changes. Haitians, Nicaraguans, Dominicans, Mexicans, Indonesians, Cambodians, East Indians, Chinese and Vietnamese bring their own innovative foods and flavors to Florida.

Florida is truly the birthplace of American cooking. Come join me then on a culi-nary tour of Florida. You won't be sorry you came for the ride!

Enjoy,

Angela E. Spenceley

 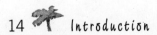

Tropical Snacks, First Courses and Appetizers

NATIVE FLORIDIAN CUISINE is really a cornucopia of foods: the everyday kind you see on your grocer's shelves, and the exotic kind with names such as guava, papaya or calamondin (cross between a kumquat and a tangerine).

Until I moved to Miami, I didn't realize Florida grew much of the produce consumed in the Northern states, strawberries, tomatoes, celery, beans just to name a few. However, the state also farms little known produce such as plantain (banana family), cassava, malanga, chayote, mango, sapodilla, passion fruit, ackee, calabaza and others.

The appetizers featured in this section are fun, delightful recipes that include such local specialties as Conch Fritters served with Mango-Mustard Sauce, smoked fish, stoned crab claws and *bollos*, Cuban black-eyed pea fritters. You'll find a number of different dips and sauces for appetizers that can also be used in recipes for fish, poultry, meat and vegetables.

So take your time and flip through this cookbook. See what interesting combinations you can come up with. After all, this is how great recipes and cooks are born!

THE RECIPES

KEY LARGO CONCH FRITTERS WITH TOMATO-CAPER COCKTAIL SAUCE

This recipe, indigenous to the upper Keys, has a firm, slightly chewy texture nice for a light lunch. Serve with a green salad and ice-cold beer.

Region: The Keys
Yield: about 20 to 25 fritters

Conch fritters figure importantly in Key West cooking, as well as the rest of the Caribbean. These tiny fried croquettes of ground conch, bread crumbs, herbs and vegetables can be found as far south as Aruba. Since they freeze well, double the recipe, and reheat for spur of the moment guests. This recipe, indigenous to the Upper Keys, has a firm texture, slightly chewy texture nice for a light lunch, served with a green side salad, and ice-cold beer.

1 1/4 pounds conch, cleaned (see sidebar, page 19) and run through a food processor
8 ounces plain bread crumbs
3 small eggs, lightly beaten
1 small stalk celery, finely chopped
1 red bell pepper, finely chopped
1 medium yellow onion, finely chopped
2 tablespoons chopped fresh parsley, preferably flat-leafed; or 2 tablespoons dried
1 tablespoon chopped fresh thyme, or 1 teaspoon dried
1/2 teaspoon paprika
2 tablespoons cider vinegar
3 tablespoons water
1/2 teaspoon grated fresh lime rind
1/2 teaspoon salt
1/2 teaspoon fresh cracked black pepper
1/4 teaspoon cayenne pepper
3 tablespoons Tabasco™
3/4 cup crushed Saltine™ crackers
vegetable oil for frying

1. Place conch, bread crumbs, eggs, celery, bell pepper, onion, parsley, thyme, paprika, vinegar, water, lime rind, salt, cayenne, black pepper and Tabasco© in food processor. Grind until well combined, then transfer to a large bowl.

2. Heat oil in a deep skillet over medium-high heat to 350º.

3. Wet hands, scoop up golf-ball sized balls and flatten slightly. Roll in crushed crackers. Fry fritters three at a time (do not over load skillet, as this will reduce heat of oil, causing the fritters to become greasy), four to five minutes on each side, or until golden.

4. Drain on white paper towels. Serve with cocktail sauce. NOTE: Do not use printed paper towels. I prefer to use the kind indicated for food usage, such as the kind that specify microwave safe.

TOMATO-CAPER COCKTAIL SAUCE
Yield: about 1 1/2 cups

I upgraded this simple sauce by using fresh horseradish. The capers add an interesting tang. You can substitute prepared white horseradish for the fresh, but it won't be as zippy.

- 1 cup ketchup
- 2 tablespoons grated horseradish
- 1 tablespoons capers, finely chopped
- 1 tablespoon chopped fresh cilantro
- 2 tablespoons fresh Key lime or lime juice
- 1 tablespoon Worcestershire™ sauce
- 1 teaspoon Tabasco™
- 1/2 teaspoon fresh cracked black pepper

1. Combine ketchup, horseradish, capers, cilantro, lime juice, Worcestershire™, Tabasco™ and black pepper in a small bowl.

2. Cover and refrigerate until thoroughly chilled. Serve with conch fritters.

THE BEST CONCH FRITTERS EVER WITH MANGO-MUSTARD SAUCE

Region: The Keys
Yield: about 20 fritters

Light, fluffy and bursting with herbs and spices, serve with Mango-Mustard Sauce that follows.

- 1 cup whole milk
- 2 teaspoons balsamic vinegar
- 1/2 teaspoon ground cumin
- 1/4 teaspoon ground nutmeg, divided
- 1 pound conch, cleaned, and sliced
- 1 large onion, quartered
- 1 small red bell pepper, seeded and quartered
- 1 small green bell pepper, seeded and quartered
- 1 small stalk celery, diced
- 2 cups all-purpose flour
- 1 tablespoon baking soda
- 1 tablespoon baking powder
- 1/4 teaspoon ground cumin
- 1/8 teaspoon ground nutmeg
- 1 teaspoon chopped fresh basil, or 1/2 teaspoon dried
- 1/2 teaspoon fresh cracked black pepper
- 1/2 cup whole milk
- 3 small eggs, lightly beaten
- 1 tablespoon Tabasco™
- 1 tablespoon butter
vegetable oil for frying

CONCH

Conch, pronounced 'konk', is a spiral-shaped gastropod, resembling a giant snail found off the coasts of Florida, Gulf coasts and the Caribbean. Conch is tough and requires tenderizing before use. It can be eaten raw, like a salad, if marinated. West coast cooks may substitute abalone for conch.

*Purchase: Conch can be purchased in the shell, or if you're lucky enough to find it, frozen, whole or ground in some gourmet grocers.

*Removing from shell: Here are few popular methods I found in the Keys: **A:** Place in freezer for 48 hours, remove and defrost in cold water until thawed, conch can then be readily removed from its shell; or **B:** Scrub outer shell under cold, running water, place in a deep kettle, cover with water, bring to boil, adding a tablespoon of salt and 1/3 cup of fresh lemon juice. Boil for three to four minutes. When conch has gone back into its shell, remove from boiling water, then drain in a metal colander (plastic will melt from the heat) under cool running water. Conch can then be removed from shell with a long strong fork, such as the kind used for barbequing; or **C:** Place conch on a large, heavy wood cutting board, the conch's opening side down. At the top of the spiral, measure down about two inches, and puncture using an ice pick and a hammer. Jam ice pick inside, and twist to get the conch free. Pick up shell, open side down, and conch will fall out. Pry with ice pick if needed.

To can: Not all of the conch muscle is edible. Using a sharp knife, slice off the orange mantle, eyes and darker area adjacent to foot. Devein, then make vertical scores through skin, and peel off outer membrane. Rinse under cool running water.

To tenderize: The meat from these large snails is extremely tough. I remember having conch chowder as a teenager on Back Street in St. Thomas in the U.S. Virgin Islands. Tomato-based, fragrant and spicy, inevitably there would be just one impossibly chewy piece of conch not finely chopped enough. **A:** The conch purchased in gourmet stores is usually sold tenderized, so no further treatment is needed. **B:** Conch may be run through a food grinder or food processor. No tenderizing necessary then. **C:** Pound with a mallet to break up the tough tendons. **D:** Slice conch thinly, place in kettle, cover with cold water and bring to boil. Reduce heat at once, and simmer for one and a half to two hours. **E:** Marinate 1 pound of thinly sliced conch in 1/2 cup lime juice, 1/2 cup cider vinegar and 1 tablespoon balsamic vinegar for 24 hours to "cook", i.e. pickle.

1. Combine milk and vinegar in a small bowl. Allow to sit for 15 minutes to sour milk.

2. Toast cumin and 1/8 teaspoon nutmeg in a small skillet over medium heat until slightly darkened and fragrant. Remove from heat and set aside.

3. Grind conch, onions, bell peppers and celery in a food processor or mill until finely chopped. Set aside.

4. Mix together, flour, baking soda, baking powder, cumin, 1/8 teaspoon nutmeg, basil and black pepper in a large, heavy bowl.

5. Fold in ground conch mixture, milk, eggs, and Tabasco™ until well combined.

6. Heat vegetable oil to 350°. Drop in 1 tablespoon butter. Wet hands and scoop up a golf-ball sized mound of conch mixture. Form into slightly flattened patties and drop three at time into hot fat. Fry for three to four minutes until golden.

7. Drain on white paper towels. When cooked, break open to test for doneness. Serve with Mango Mustard Sauce or Tomato-Caper Cocktail Sauce.

MANGO-MUSTARD SAUCE
Yield: about 1 cup

- 1/2 cup Dijon-style mustard
- 1/2 cup good-quality Mango chutney or Mango preserves (peach or apricot may be substituted)
- juice of 1 lime (2 tablespoons)
- 1 tablespoon grated fresh horseradish, or 1 tablespoon prepared white horseradish
- 1/2 teaspoon cayenne pepper

1. Combine all ingredients in a small bowl. Cover and refrigerate overnight to allow flavors to mingle.

2. Remove from refrigerator, bringing to room temperature. Serve with piping hot conch fritters.

CRACKED GARLIC CONCH

Region: The Keys
Yield: 4 to 6 servings

I'm a huge fan of garlic, and I've tripled the amount of garlic required in the original recipe. Garlic is excellent for high blood pressure. Try and buy firm, unblemished heads of garlic, avoiding any that appear shriveled or have brown spots. I purchased organic garlic the other day. Whew! It was as spicy as horseradish. That told me how old the stuff was from the supermarket.

4 conch, removed from shell and cleaned
1/2 cup fresh Key lime or lime juice
1/4 cup fresh lemon juice
2 tablespoon cider vinegar
1/2 cup seasoned bread crumbs
4 to 5 cloves garlic, crushed
1 tablespoon Tabasco™
1 1/2 teaspoons chopped fresh basil or
    1/2 teaspoon dried
1/4 teaspoon dried thyme
3 small eggs, lightly beaten
1 tablespoon Worcestershire™ sauce
1/2 cup all-purpose flour
vegetable oil for frying
lemon or lime wedges

1. Pound conch with a wooden mallet until it is so thin it looks like lace.

2. Place conch in a non-reactive or glass-baking dish. Pour lime and lemon juice, and vinegar over the top. Cover and marinate overnight in the refrigerator.

3. Combine bread crumbs, garlic, Tabasco™, basil and thyme in a small bowl. Whisk beaten eggs with Worcestershire™ in a second bowl. Place flour in a third bowl.

4. Heat oil to 375º in a large, heavy skillet.

5. Dip the conch into the beaten eggs, then dredge in flour, then dip in eggs again, then roll in bread crumbs.

6. Carefully lower into hot fat, looking out for splatters. Fry until for four to five minutes, until crunchy and golden.

7. Drain on white paper towels.

8. Serve with Mango-Mustard Sauce, Mango Chutney or Tomato-Caper Sauce, along with lemon or lime wedges.

DID YOU KNOW?

On April 18, 1982, the United States Border Patrol set up a blockade at the top of the only highway going in and out of the **Florida Keys.** Their intention was to apprehend illegal aliens. All of the Keys were treated as a foreign country, and anyone entering or leaving had to prove U.S. citizenship.

On April 23, 1982, **Key West** in a mock ceremony, declared its independence from the United States and called itself **The Conch Republic.**

CONCH CEVICHE WITH SESAME SOY SAUCE

Region: Miami, Gold Coast
Yield: 6 to 8 servings

I like to serve this on summer days, when it is just too hot to eat anything but chilled food.

- 1 1/2 pounds, cleaned conch
- 2 tomatoes, peeled, seeded and cut in thin wedges
- 1 medium onion, thinly sliced
- 1 green bell pepper, sliced in strips
- 1 small rib stalk celery, sliced thinly on diagonal
- juice of 3 limes (3 tablespoons)
- 4 tablespoons cider vinegar, divided
- 3 tablespoons tamari or soy sauce
- 2 tablespoons water
- 1 tablespoon balsamic vinegar
- juice of 1 lime (2 tablespoons)
- 1 teaspoon Dijon-style mustard
- 1 tablespoon toasted sesame oil
- 1/2 cup olive oil
- 3 tablespoons Tupelo honey (substitute regular honey)
- 1 garlic clove, crushed

1. Slice cleaned conch thinly by hand or food processor. Place in non-reactive bowl with tomatoes, onion, bell pepper and celery. Pour 3 tablespoons lime juice and 2 tablespoons of the cider vinegar over top and toss to combine. Refrigerate overnight, or eight hours.

2. Place remaining cider vinegar, tamari, water, balsamic vinegar, 2 tablespoons lime juice and mustard in a food processor or blender. Blend, then slowly add sesame and olive oil a little bit at a time, with blender running. Finally add honey and garlic; puree until smooth. Cover and refrigerate for two hours. Serve as a dipping sauce for conch.

DEEP-FRIED CRAB FINGERS

Region: Gulf Coast
Yield: 6 to 8 servings

There are two types of edible crab found in Florida waters: blue crab, a.k.a. soft-shell crab (caught when the old shell is shed, and the new one has not fully formed); and stone crab. These sizzling crab fingers are highly addictive, making a perfect appetizer or finger food for that special party.

- 2 pounds steamed, blue crab fingers (see sidebar for cooking)
- 2 large eggs, lightly beaten
- 1 cup finely ground cornmeal
- 1 cup all-purpose flour

1 1/2 teaspoons chopped fresh basil, or 1/2 teaspoon dried

1/4 teaspoon dried thyme

1/4 teaspoon cayenne pepper

1/2 teaspoon salt

1/2 teaspoon fresh cracked black pepper

vegetable oil for frying

1. Place beaten eggs in a small bowl. In a second bowl, combine cornmeal, flour, basil, thyme, cayenne, salt and black pepper.

2. Remove shells from crab fingers by placing a sharp knife near the pincer, tapping with a mallet or hammer until shell cracks. Slip off shell carefully, reserving the pincer as a handle for the crabmeat.

3. Using pincers as a handle, dip crabmeat into eggs, then flour mixture, tapping off excess.

4. Line a glass or ceramic baking dish with sheets of white paper towel. I prefer to use white paper towels (bleached without the use of chlorine) that I find at the health food store. Regular paper towels are treated with formaldehyde to improve their strength when wet.

5. Heat 1-inch of oil a deep skillet to 350º. Carefully lower fingers, three at a time into hot fat. Fry until golden, about three to four minutes. Remove from oil, draining on white paper towels. Place in a warm oven, approximate 200º until all fingers are fried.

6. Serve with Tomato-Caper Cocktail Sauce.

BLUE CRAB

Blue crabs are found in bays and estuaries. I've seen then migrate across roads, many miles from water. White lump meat is used in recipes, and the claws steamed or fried.

Purchase: Never purchase or cook unless the crab's legs are still moving. Hold crab by its pincers, near the rear to avoid painful accidents.

Steaming: *You'll need 36 live crabs.* Combine 1/2 cup seafood seasoning, such as Old Bay™, with 1/2 cup salt, 3 cups white vinegar (use the kind sold in a glass bottle—the acid in vinegar leaches chemicals from the plastic), 3 cups beer in a very large kettle with a rack and a tight fitting lid. Add crabs on top of the rack, turn heat on medium high, and steam for 20 minutes until crabs turn orange.

CRAB CAKES WITH DILLED TARTAR SAUCE

Region: Gulf Coast
Yield: 6 servings

I can't think of anyone who doesn't love crab cakes, unless they're made with too many bread crumbs and not enough crabmeat. The Parmesan cheese adds a welcome piquancy. Serve with Dilled Tartar Sauce or Mango-Mustard Chutney, and plenty of lime or lemon wedges.

> 1 pound cooked blue crab meat
> 3/4 cup plain bread crumbs
> 1/4 cup grated Parmesan cheese
> 1/2 teaspoon salt
> 1/2 teaspoon fresh cracked black pepper
> 2 garlic cloves, crushed
> 2 large eggs, lightly beaten
> 1/4 cup mayonnaise
> 2 tablespoons sour cream
> 1/4 cup chopped fresh parsley
> 2 tablespoons finely chopped yellow onion
> 2 tablespoons fresh lime or lemon juice
> 1 teaspoon Worcestershire™ sauce
> 1/4 teaspoon paprika
> vegetable oil for frying

1. Flake crabmeat into a small bowl. Set aside.

2. Combine bread crumbs, Parmesan, salt, black pepper, garlic, eggs, mayonnaise, sour cream, parsley, onion, lime juice, Worcestershire™ and paprika in a medium bowl. Fold in crabmeat. If mixture is too dry, stir in whole milk by the tablespoon, until six patties can be formed.

3. Place patties on waxed paper and refrigerate for at least one hour.

4. Heat 1-inch of vegetable oil to 350° in a large, heavy skillet. Drop patties in hot oil, three at a time, frying five minutes on each side until golden.

5. Drain on white paper towels. Serve with Dilled Tartar Sauce, hot French fries, coleslaw or a green salad.

NOTE: Some recipes call for butter instead of vegetable oil for frying. I find it burns too easily. If you like the flavor of butter, add a couple of tablespoons to your frying oil.

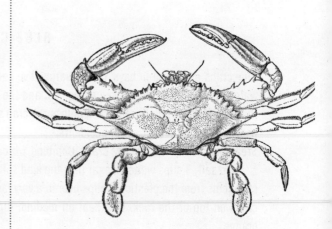

DILLED TARTAR SAUCE
Yield: a little over 1 1/2 cups

Bottled tartar sauce is readily available, but why bother when you can make fresh in no time at all?

- 1 cup mayonnaise
- 1/4 cup sour cream
- 1/2 cup sweet pickle relish
- 3 tablespoons finely chopped onion
- 1 clove garlic, crushed
- 1 tablespoon chopped fresh dill, or 1 1/2 teaspoons dried
- 1 teaspoon Tabasco™

1. Combine all ingredients in a small bowl. Cover and refrigerate for several hours.

2. Serve as a dipping sauce with piping hot crab cakes.

ISLAND-STYLE CRAB DIP

Region: Florida—Caribbean
Yield: about 4 cups

It was really difficult for me to complete this cookbook. Halfway through I had gained so much weight, I ended up spending two hours a day at the gym, which cut into my kitchen time considerably. This recipe is a wonderful way to use up any leftover crabmeat, or shrimp. Refrigerate overnight, at least eight hours, for peak melding of flavors. Keeps up to two days in the refrigerator.

- 1/2 pound cooked, flaked crabmeat
- 1 medium onion, finely chopped
- 1 large stalk celery, diced
- 1 clove garlic, crushed
- 1/2 small jalapeño pepper, seeded and finely chopped
- 1 (3-ounce) package cream cheese, softened
- 3/4 cup mayonnaise
- 1/4 cup sour cream
- 3 tablespoons chopped fresh parsley
- 1 teaspoon Old Bay™ seafood seasoning
- 1/2 teaspoon fresh cracked black pepper

1. Pick over crab, discarding any bones or cartilage. Set aside. Chop into bite-size pieces. Set aside.

2. Blend onion, celery, garlic, jalapeño pepper, cream cheese, mayonnaise, sour cream, parsley, Old Bay™ and black pepper in a food processor until smooth. Remove blade from food processor, and fold in crab by hand.

3. Cover and refrigerate for several hours. To serve, place bowl inside a larger bowl filled with crushed ice to keep dip cool and appealing. Serve with Saltines™

GARLICKY CHEESE AND CRAB DIP

Region: Miami, Gold Coast
Yield: 6 to 8 servings

This dip won't take up much of your time to prepare. Fresh crabmeat is best, but keep several high-quality tins of canned on hand for emergencies.

1 pound cooked blue crabmeat, or 3 (6-ounce) cans crabmeat
1 cup grated Swiss cheese
1 medium onion, finely chopped
1 small stalk celery, diced
4 cloves garlic, crushed
3/4 cup mayonnaise
1 (3-ounce package) cream cheese, softened
14 sour cream

1 tablespoon Tabasco™
1 teaspoon Old Bay™ seafood seasoning
1 large tomato, thinly sliced
Saltines™

1. Preheat oven to 350°.

2. Pick over crabmeat for bones and cartilage. Set aside.

3. Combine Swiss cheese, onion, celery, garlic, mayonnaise, cream cheese, sour cream, Tabasco™ and Old Bay™ seasoning in a large bowl. Fold in crabmeat.

4. Spoon into a 11/2 quart ceramic or glass-baking dish. Top with tomato slices. Bake for 30 minutes.

5. Serve hot in same dish with crisp crackers.

STONE CRABS

With their large red and black claws, stone crabs are a Florida staple. Only the claws are removed for eating when the crabs are caught. The crab is then tossed back into the water, where he will grow a new claw in about eighteen months.

Purchasing: Claws cooked to order are indeed a luxury. Crab claws are cooked soon after they are caught because crabs periodically outgrow their shells. The old shell is discarded, and a new larger shell forms, while they continue to grow on the inside. When a crabber brings his booty to the seafood wholesaler, the claws are submerged in boiling water. Any claws that float, i.e. because they don't have enough meat inside, are discarded. The claws that sink, are full of meat, and sold at market. Occasionally in the Keys, you'll find an outdoor vendor selling crab claws at half market price. These are called lights. Kind of a bargain, twice as many claws will have to be cracked to attain enough meat.

HOT STONE CRABS WITH MELTED GARLIC BUTTER

Region: The Keys
Yield: 4 servings

- 1 tablespoon olive oil
- 6 garlic cloves, crushed
- 1 teaspoon sea salt
- 1/2 teaspoon fresh cracked black pepper
- 3/4 cup (1 1/2 sticks) melted butter
- 1/8 teaspoon ground nutmeg
- 1/8 teaspoon cayenne pepper
- 16 cooked stone crab claws

1. Heat olive oil in a medium skillet. Sauté garlic until soft. Remove from heat, stir in sea salt and black pepper. Set aside.

2. Reheat cooked claws for about eight minutes in boiling water. Remove from water, and allow to drain. Crack each of the three joints with a wooden mallet.

3. Stir in garlic mixture to melted butter. Sprinkle with nutmeg and cayenne. Divide into four small dipping bowls, serving alongside claws.

CHILLED STONE CRAB CLAWS WITH CHARDONNAY MUSTARD SAUCE

Region: The Keys
Yield: about 1 1/4 cups

Delicious as an special appetizer or light lunch course.

- 1/4 cup Chardonnay
- 1/4 cup Dijon-style mustard
- 1/4 cup sour cream
- 1/4 cup mayonnaise
- 2 tablespoons Worcestershire™ sauce
- 1 tablespoon finely chopped onion
- 1/2 cup light cream
- 1/2 teaspoon paprika
- juice of 1 lime (2 tablespoons)
- 16 cooked stone crab claws, chilled

1. Combine Chardonnay, mustard, sour cream, mayonnaise, Worcestershire™ and onion in a small bowl.

2. Beat in light cream and paprika using a hand mixer set at low speed until mixture thickens. Cover and refrigerate for two hours.

3. Just before serving, stir in lime juice. Arrange crab claws on a serving dish alongside the Chardonnay Mustard Sauce.

FIERY CARIBBEAN LOBSTER FRITTERS

Region: Florida—Caribbean
Yield: about 4 servings

If the fire of the habañero pepper is too hot for you, substitute slightly milder jalapeños, or douse the fire instead using a green bell pepper

- 1 pound lobster meat
- 1/4 cup all-purpose flour, sifted
- 1 tablespoon finely ground cornmeal
- 3 eggs, beaten
- 1/2 cup whole milk
- 1/2 cup light cream
- 1 tablespoon Tabasco™
- 1/2 teaspoon fresh cracked black pepper
- 1/2 teaspoon salt
- 1 small habañero, or 1 small green bell pepper, finely chopped
- vegetable oil for frying

1. Pick over lobster meat for cartilage and bones. Dice meat finely. Set aside.

2. Fold eggs into flour and cornmeal. Whisk in milk, cream and Tabasco™. Stir in black pepper and salt. Beat until smooth, then cut in hot peppers.

3. Heat 1-inch of oil in a large skillet to 350°.

4. Add lobster meat to batter, combining well.

5. Drop batter by large spoonfuls into hot fat. Do not overcrowd as this will reduce temperature of oil and cause the fritters to absorb too much oil. Fry until golden.

6. Drain on food-grade white paper towels (those that are suitable for microwaving are fine).

NOTE: Do not put fingers in eyes after handling habañero pepper as a burn will result.

OYSTER PIE

Region: Northeast, Fernandina Beach
Yield: 4 to 6 servings

During oyster season, (fall and winter) you'll find notices of oyster roasts posted in this historic town. At many local homes, you'll find stone tables used just to roast oysters.

- 2 (9-inch) pie crust shells (unbaked)
- 2 slices uncooked bacon
- 1 tablespoon olive oil
- 2 tablespoons all-purpose flour
- 1/2 cup whole milk
- 1/4 cup evaporated milk (unsweetened)
- 1 quart shucked oysters with liquid reserved

1 teaspoons Worcestershire™ sauce
1/2 teaspoon Cajun seasoning
1 1/2 teaspoons chopped fresh thyme or 1/2
teaspoon dried
1 1/2 teaspoons chopped fresh marjoram or 1/2
teaspoon dried
1/2 teaspoon salt
1/2 teaspoon fresh cracked black pepper
2 tablespoons dry sherry

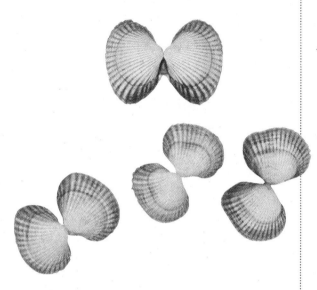

1. Preheat oven to 375° F. Place bacon in a large, heavy skillet. Brown evenly on all sides. Remove from pan, crumble and set aside, draining on white paper towels. Reserve 1 tablespoon of fat.

2. Heat bacon fat and olive oil over medium heat. Sprinkle in flour, stirring constantly for 10 minutes to make a light brown roux. Gradually beat in milks and 1 cup of oyster liquid. Cook until thick and gravy-like.

3. Add Worcestershire™, Cajun seasoning, thyme, marjoram, salt, black pepper, sherry and oysters. Pour mixture into 9-inch pie shell and top with remaining crust.

4. Bake for 30 minutes, until golden.

SMOKED MARLIN SPREAD

Region: The Keys
Yield: about 8 servings

Fish smoked in the Keys is first soaked overnight in a solution made up of salt, brown sugar, and spices. It's an intricate process using a smoke house, which resembles a tall dresser of drawers. Any type of smoked fish may be substituted for the Marlin

1 pound smoked Marlin, skin and bones removed
1 (8-ounce) package cream cheese softened, cut in chunks
2 tablespoons mayonnaise
1 tablespoon sour cream
2 tablespoons prepared white horseradish
1/4 cup finely chopped yellow onion
3 tablespoons chopped fresh parsley, or 1 tablespoon dried

1 tablespoon chopped fresh cilantro, or 1
  teaspoon dried
1 tablespoon fresh Key lime or lime juice
1 tablespoon Worcestershire™
1 teaspoon Tabasco™
1/2 teaspoon paprika

1. Coarsely flake fish, removing any pieces of bones or skin.

2. Combine fish, cream cheese, mayonnaise, sour cream, horseradish, onion, parsley, cilantro, lime juice, Worcestershire™, Tabasco™ and paprika in a food processor until smooth. Refrigerate for several hours until well chilled.

3. Serve as a dip for raw vegetables, crusty bread or crackers.

BOLLOS (BLACK-EYED PEA FRITTERS)

Region: Miami—Cuban
Yield: 30 to 40 *bollos*

Bollos can be found in Cuban restaurants and other eateries in Key West, but interestingly not in Miami. Bollos make a great side dish, or an appetizer served with chilled beer. If you don't have time to soak and cook peas, use the canned kind.

2 cups dried black-eyed peas
1 medium onion, quartered
4 large cloves of garlic, crushed
1 small jalapeño or 1/2 habañero pepper, carefully seeded and finely chopped
1 tablespoon chopped fresh cilantro
3/4 teaspoon salt
1/2 teaspoon fresh cracked black pepper
1/2 cup flour
2 tablespoons finely ground cornmeal
vegetable oil for frying
salt
pepper

1. Soak peas overnight. Drain, rinse and bring to a boil in a medium saucepan. Lower heat to a simmer, cover and cook for two hours until soft. Drain and cool slightly. If using canned peas, rinse and drain.

DID YOU KNOW?

The best use for a panoramic camera is the **Seven-Mile Bridge** (actually 6.79 miles long), which connects the **Middle** and **Lower Keys**. Considered the world's longest segmental bridge, it has 39 expansion joints, dividing each cement section. Each year, in April, runners gather in Marathon (in the Middle Keys) for the Seven-Mile-Bridge Run.

2. Place peas in a food processor along with onion, garlic, hot pepper, cilantro, salt and black pepper. Puree until smooth.

3. Combine flour and cornmeal in a small bowl. Wet hands, dip hands into pea mixture and form golf-ball-sized balls. Roll in flour mixture, lightly shaking off excess.

4. Heat 1-inch of oil in a large skillet to 350°. Gingerly lower bollos into hot fat. Fry for one to two minutes until golden. Drain on food-grade white paper towels. Serve hot, seasoning to taste with salt and black pepper.

FROMAJARDIS—CHEESE PASTRIES

Region: Northeast—St. Augustine
Yield: 10 to 24, depending on size

The Spanish explorer Ponce de León landed just a bit south of the St. Mary's River in 1513. León and his men subsisted on corn, beans, squash, hearts of palm (swamp cabbage) and fish supplied by the natives. Fifty-two years later, St. Augustine, the oldest city in the United States, was founded as a Spanish mission. The nuns and priests took advantage of the wild boar brought over by the Spanish conquistadors, and combined the pork meat with a variety of wild fruits, vegetables, small game and fish. Two hundred years later, Minorcans (immigrants from Greece, Italy and the island of Minorca originally brought over as indentured servants to work an indigo plantation), settled in St. Augustine and introduced Mediterranean flavors to the city.

Traditionally, Minorcan women bake Fromjardis shortly before Easter. The night before Easter, carolers serenade the streets, and tap the shutters of Minorcan homes. In turn, the host would offer up these crispy cheese pastries. This custom is still observed in some parts of St. Augustine at Easter.

3¼ cups all-purpose flour
1¼ teaspoons salt
1 teaspoon sugar
¼ teaspoon ground cardamom
¼ teaspoon ground black pepper
¼ cup solid vegetable shortening
¼ cup (½ stick) firm butter, chopped in pieces
10 tablespoons cold water
5 medium eggs
½ pound sharp Cheddar cheese, grated
1 teaspoon Datil pepper, finely chopped, or other hot chili pepper (use more or less to taste)

1. Sift the flour, salt, sugar, cardamom and black pepper into a large bowl.

Divide shortening in half and cut into flour with a pastry cutter or fork. Do the same with remaining shortening and the butter. The mixture will look like pebbles or coarse sand.

2. Sprinkle in water by the tablespoon until dough just clings together. You will need more or less water depending upon the moisture content of the flour.

3. Roll dough into a ball and wrap with plastic. Refrigerate. Preheat oven to 400°F. Whisk together eggs, cheese and hot pepper. Set aside.

4. Divide dough in half. Roll 1/8-inch thick. Cut out rounds three to six inches in diameter. I flip a small plastic mixing bowl or plastic food container upside down to do this.

5. Drop cheese filling by teaspoonfuls onto rounds (one teaspoon for small pastries; two to three for large). Fold over, pinching edges together, turnover-style. Score tops with the tip of a sharp knife. Bake on ungreased cookie sheets on center oven rack for 10 to 12 minutes until golden and crisp. Best served hot from oven.

CAUTION: Datil peppers are scorching hot. Start with a small amount, tasting first.

LEMON-SALMON PIZZA

Region: Miami—Gold Coast
Yield: 8 servings

- 1/2 cup sour cream
- 1/2 cup heavy cream
- 1 (3-ounce package) cream cheese, softened
- 1 tablespoon chopped fresh basil
- 1 garlic clove, crushed
- 1 lemon
- 1 (10 to 12-inch) pre-baked pizza crust
- 4 to 6 ounces smoked salmon
- 3/4 cup shredded mozzarella cheese
- 1/2 cup grated Parmesan cheese
- 1 tablespoon dried Italian herbs

1. Combine sour cream, heavy cream, cream cheese, basil and garlic in a small bowl. Allow to stand at room temperature for one hour.

2. Preheat oven to 450° F.

3. Wash outside of lemon with soap and water. Peel off yellow rind, and slice very thinly, removing all seeds.

4. Arrange lemon slices on pizza crust, then place on baking sheet.

5. Bake for 9 to 10 minutes. Lemon slices will be crunchy, but not burnt.

6. Slice smoked salmon in 1-inch strips.

Arrange over lemon slices. Spread sour cream over salmon.

7. Combine mozzarella, Parmesan and herbs in a small bowl. Sprinkle over sour cream.

8. Return to oven and bake until cheese is lightly browned and bubbly.

SPICY HAVANA PLANTAIN CHIPS

Region: Maimi—Cuban
Yield: 4 to 6 servings

    4 to 5 green plantains
    1 lemon or lime, halved
vegetable oil for frying
    1 small garlic clove, crushed
    1 teaspoon salt or garlic salt
1/2 teaspoon cayenne pepper
1/2 teaspoon ground black pepper
1/2 teaspoon paprika

1. Peel plantains by slicing off one end of fruit with a sharp knife, grabbing peel between thumb and knife, and pulling.

2. Rub plantain with lemon to keep from turning brown. Slice plantains very thin, like potato chips.

3. Heat 1-inch of oil so that it begins to dance in a large skillet. Do not allow to smoke—that is too hot. Sauté garlic for 30 seconds.

4. Fry plantain slices in small batches until golden. Do not overcrowd pan.

5. Remove with slotted spoon and drain on white paper towels.

6. Combine salt, cayenne, paprika and black pepper. Sprinkle over chips to taste.

DID YOU KNOW?

Miami rests on a paved swamp between the Everglades and Atlantic Ocean. Decidedly Latin in flavor, Miami is divided into four quadrants, northeast, northwest, southeast and southwest. Most people envision glitzy nightlife, palms and sunshine when they think of Miami. There's a lot more to this tropical city than million-dollar high-rises and flashy South Beach clubs. From swank Bal Harbour shops, ethnic eateries, secluded five-star hotels, to quiet areas in the north such as Sunny Isles Beach, Miami offers something for everyone, young or old.

Sunshine Soups, Chowders, and Bisques

THE ABUNDANCE OF FISH and shellfish in Florida lends itself to a dazzling array of soups and chowders.

Of all the parts of a meal, soup is the most versatile. It can be an elegant first course designed to whet your appetite to a chunky hearty stew that serves as a main meal.

Most soups last a few days in the refrigerator and actually taste better the next day. Many soups freeze well. If you're a weekend cook and want to get a jump on the week's menus, soup is an excellent investment of your time.

The secret to a superior fish chowder lies in the quality of the stock used. Whenever possible, take the time to make a homemade stock as it makes a huge difference in the end product. Make a double batch and freeze extras. If you are really pressed for time, some of the mail order kitchen gourmet shops sell a jarred, high-quality stock base, which I've used successfully.

In this chapter, you'll find everything from tomato-based chowder, creamy bisques to zesty black bean soup.

THE RECIPES

TOMATO-BASIL CONCH CHOWDER

Region: The Keys
Yield: 6 to 8 servings

The addition of basil adds a lively kick to this conch chowder. Omit basil for traditional Tomato-Based Conch Chowder.

 1 pound conch, cleaned (substitute clams or abalone if desired)
1/4 pound salt pork or bacon, chopped
 1 medium onion, finely chopped
 2 large cloves garlic, crushed
 1 large stalk celery, diced
 2 quarts water
 1 cup clam juice
 2 medium carrots, peeled and diced
 1 (14.5-ounce) can peeled tomatoes, coarsely chopped and juice reserved
 3 tablespoons tomato paste
 1 tablespoon chopped fresh basil, or 1 teaspoon dried
 2 large potatoes, peeled and cut into 1/2 inch pieces
 1 teaspoon dried thyme
 2 tablespoons Tabasco™
1/4 cup dry white wine
1/4 cup dry sherry
  salt
  pepper

1. Pass conch through a food processor. In my opinion, conch cannot be finely chopped too fine. It's delicious, but tough unless prepared properly.

2. Brown the onion, garlic and celery with the salt pork or bacon in a deep kettle. Add water and conch. Bring to boil, reduce heat, and simmer, covered for one and a half hours.

3. Add clam juice, carrots, tomatoes and their reserved juice, tomato paste, basil, potatoes, thyme and Tabasco™, stirring to combine. Return to a boil, reduce heat, and simmer, uncovered for 25 minutes.

4. Remove from heat and stir in white wine and sherry. Season to taste with salt and pepper.

FISH STOCK

Yield: almost 2 quarts

Substitute quick and easy homemade fish stock for any part of the clam juice or water in the chowder or soup recipes for an impressive flavor boost. Keeps up to three days in the refrigerator or two months in the freezer.

8	fish heads	1	large celery stalk
6	cups water	1/2	cup parsley
2	cups dry white wine		juice of 1 lemon
2	tablespoons dry sherry	1	bay leaf
1	medium onion, sliced	1	teaspoon black peppercorns

Simmer fish heads, water, wine, sherry, onions, celery, parsley, lemon juice, bay leaf, and peppercorns in a deep kettle or stockpot for one hour. Remove from heat and strain. Stock may be refrigerated for up to four days of frozen for three months.

RICH AND CREAMY CONCH CHOWDER

Region: The Keys
Yield: about 3 quarts

1 pound conch meat, cleaned
4 cups water
2 ounces bacon or salt pork, finely chopped
2 medium yellow onions, finely chopped
1 (8-ounce) bottles clam juice
2 large stalks celery, diced
2 large potatoes, peeled and diced
1 bay leaf
1 cup whole milk
3/4 cup half-and-half

1/4 cup evaporated milk
2 tablespoons butter
salt
black pepper
paprika

1. Run conch through a food mill or processor. Fill a deep kettle or stockpot with the four cups water. Add conch, cover and simmer for one and a half hours. Remove from heat and set aside.

2. Fry bacon in a large skillet until crisp. Remove bacon bits and set aside. Fry onion until lightly browned about five minutes. Set aside.

3. Add clam juice to kettle. Stir in bacon, onions, celery, potatoes and bay leaf. Simmer, covered, for 20 minutes until potatoes are soft. Remove from heat.

4. Heat milk, half-and-half and evaporated milk in a small saucepan until hot, but not boiling.

5. Stir milk mixture into kettle (do not bring to boil). Drop in butter and season to taste with salt and black pepper. Ladle into individual bowls and sprinkle with paprika.

CONCH BISQUE

Region: The Keys
Yield: 1 1/2 quarts or about 6 servings

I adapted this recipe from an out-of-the way restaurant in Isla Morada, one of the Upper Keys. The sherry adds a nice complexity to this cream based recipe, which is lighter than the Rich and Creamy Conch Chowder recipe.

    1 pound cleaned conch
    4 cups cold water
    1 tablespoon olive oil
    1 small onion, finely chopped
    1 stalk celery, finely chopped
    3 tablespoons butter
1/4 cup all-purpose flour
1/2 teaspoon paprika
1/4 teaspoon dried thyme
    4 8-ounce bottles clam juice
1/2 cup heavy cream
1/4 cup dry sherry
    2 tablespoons chopped fresh parsley
salt
pepper

1. Run cleaned conch through a food mill or blender. Place in a deep kettle or soup pot along with the four cups water. Bring to a boil, reduce heat, cover and simmer over low heat for one and a half hours.

2. Heat olive oil in a medium skillet over moderate heat. Sauté onion and celery until onion is lightly browned and caramelized. Remove from heat and set aside.

3. Melt butter in a separate small saucepan or skillet over medium high heat. Sprinkle in flour, paprika and thyme. Stir constantly over moderate heat, until lightly browned to make a roux, which should have a nutty aroma. Stir into kettle with conch and with clam juice.

4. Bring to boil, reduce heat. Cook over low heat for 20 minutes. Remove from heat.

5. Stir in heavy cream. Stir in sherry. Season to taste with salt and pepper. Garnish with chopped parsley. Season to taste with salt and pepper.

SHRIMP AND CRAB CHOWDER

Region: The Gulf Coast
Yield: 6 to 8 servings

Pre-cooked shrimp and crab reduce kitchen time. Perfect for hectic work nights.

    1 tablespoon olive oil
    1 medium onion, finely chopped
    1 small stalk celery, finely chopped
  1/2 cup (1 stick) butter
  1/4 cup all-purpose flour
    1 teaspoon salt
  1/2 teaspoon paprika
    1 cup fish stock or 1 (8-ounce) bottle clam juice
  1/2 cup beer

 1 1/2 cups cooked crab meat, flaked and picked over
     1 cup shelled, cooked, diced shrimp
 2 1/2 cups whole milk
     2 cups light cream
   1/2 cup evaporated milk (unsweetened)
  salt
  pepper
   1/4 cup dry sherry

1. Sauté onion and celery in the olive oil in a medium skillet over moderate heat until translucent, about four to five minutes.

2. Add butter, then sprinkle in flour, stirring constantly over medium-high heat for ten minutes until lightly browned to make a roux. Stir in salt and paprika.

3. Gradually whisk in fish stock and beer, then crab and shrimp. Cover and simmer for fifteen minutes.

4. Stir in milk, light cream and evaporated milk, heating thoroughly, but not bringing to a boil. Remove from

DID YOU KNOW?

The Panhandle (northwest Florida: Pensacola, Gulf Coast, Tallahassee) with its magnolia trees and live oaks more resembles the Deep South than the rest of Florida. Some of the best beaches in Florida are here: St. Joseph Peninsula State Park, St. George Island State Park and Perdido Key State Recreation Area.

heat and season to taste with salt and pepper.

5. Ladle into individual bowls and drizzle sherry over top just before serving.

TARRAGON SHRIMP AND CABBAGE SOUP

Region: Gulf Coast
Yield: 4 to 6 servings

Be sure to use the proper shredding blade on a food processor for the cabbage. You don't want huge, chewy cabbage leaves, nor do you want mincemeat. The flavor of this soup improves the next day.

    1 medium yellow onion, finely chopped
    2 cloves garlic, crushed
    1 tablespoon olive oil
    2 tablespoons dry sherry
    5 cups shredded cabbage (1 small to medium head)
    1 stalk celery, diced
    4 cups chicken stock
    1 pound uncooked shrimp, peeled and deveined, tails on
    1 teaspoon dried tarragon
  salt
  pepper

1. Sauté onions and garlic in olive oil in a large skillet over moderate heat until translucent, five minutes. Stir constantly until lightly browned.

2. Stir in sherry; fold in cabbage and celery, cooking for two minutes over medium heat. Cabbage should be wilted, but still crisp.

3. Add chicken stock, shrimp and tarragon. Bring to a simmer and cook over low heat for 10 minutes or until shrimp are pink and cooked.

4. Season to taste with salt and pepper. Serve with crusty bread or Saltine™ crackers.

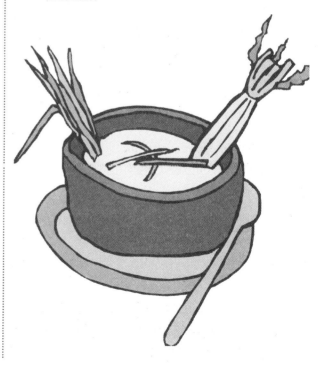

CHICKEN STOCK

Most canned chicken stocks don't have enough umpf for a tasty soup. It's really not that hard to make your own chicken stock. Freeze any extra.

1 tablespoon olive oil
1 medium onion, coarsely chopped
3 to 4 pounds chopped chicken parts
2 quarts boiling water
4 peppercorns

2 carrots
1 stalk celery
2 teaspoons salt
2 bay leaves

1. Heat oil in a deep kettle or soup pot. Sauté onion until beginning to brown. Scrape onion into a large bowl.
2. Brown one third of the chicken at a time. Return onion to kettle, add 1 cup of the boiling water, cover, and simmer on low heat for 20 minutes.
3. Add remaining boiling water, carrots, celery, salt, bay leaves and peppercorns. Bring to boil, reduce heat, cover, and simmer on low heat for 20 minutes.
4. Strain, and discard vegetables, chicken, and spices. Refrigerate up to two and a half or freeze for three months.

Yield: just under 2 quarts

CUBAN BLACK BEAN SOUP

Region: Miami—Cuban
Yield: about 8 servings

Be sure to soak the beans overnight. Drain and discard soaking water, then rinse thoroughly. This process is especially helpful for those who have trouble digesting beans.

2 cups dried black beans
4 tablespoons bacon fat
6 cloves garlic, crushed

1 medium onion, finely chopped
1 small green bell pepper, finely chopped
1 stalk celery, diced
8 cups water
3 bay leaves
1 teaspoon dried oregano
1/2 teaspoon dried thyme
1/2 teaspoon ground cumin
1 tablespoon hot pepper sauce, such as Tabasco™ or habañero sauce
1/4 cup cider vinegar
2 teaspoons sugar
2 hard-cooked eggs, chopped
1/2 cup finely chopped onion

2 tablespoons chopped fresh cilantro
salt
fresh cracked black pepper
hot rice

1. Place beans in a large bowl, cover with cold water and soak overnight. Drain and rinse.

2. Sauté onion, garlic and bell pepper in bacon fat in a deep kettle or soup pot. Add water, bay leaves, oregano, thyme and cumin. Bring to a boil, reduce heat, cover and simmer for two hours until beans are soft.

4. Remove from heat, stir in hot sauce, vinegar and sugar. Season to taste with salt and black pepper.

5. Ladle into individual bowls and garnish with chopped onion, eggs and cilantro. Serve with hot rice.

NOTE: You can substitute olive oil for the bacon fat.

PUMPKIN WITH CHICKEN SOUP

Region: Florida—Caribbean
Yield: 6 servings

This recipe was given to me many years ago by my children's nanny in St. Thomas. I shared it with my new Cuban housekeeper in Miami, who added her own native herbs and spices. I particularly enjoyed the addition of dark rum.

- 1 (3-4) pound pumpkin, peeled, seeded and cut in 1-inch cubes
- 2 tablespoons olive oil
- 1 medium yellow onion, finely chopped
- 3 cloves garlic, crushed
- 2 stalks celery, diced
- 1/2 teaspoon dried oregano
- 1/2 teaspoon dried thyme
- 1/2 teaspoon ground cumin
- 4 cups chicken stock
- 1 1/2 cups diced, cooked chicken meat
- 1 cup light cream
- salt
- pepper

1. Place pumpkin in a large kettle and add 1-inch of water. Cover and bring to boil, steaming pumpkin for 10 to 12 minutes, until soft. Add small amounts of water as needed. Remove from heat, and reserve any cooking water (full of nutrients). Cool.

2. Puree pumpkin in batches in a food processor, adding reserved pumpkin water and chicken stock as needed. Return to kettle and set aside.

3. Sauté the onion, garlic and celery in the olive oil over moderate heat in a medium skillet until onion is lightly browned. Add to pumpkin, cooking and stirring occasionally for 10 minutes.

4. Stir in oregano, thyme, cumin and any remaining chicken stock. Bring to a boil, reduce heat. Fold in diced chicken and simmer for five minutes until heated through.

5. Remove from heat and fold in light cream.

6. Season to taste with salt (you may not need any because of the sodium content in the chicken stock) and black pepper.

Cooling Salads and Light Fare

FLORIDA RESTAURANTS AND CHEFS are famous for their ingenious use of local produce in salads. Many of these first courses, like the soups in the preceding chapter, are meals in themselves. Serve with crispy flatbreads, crusty French bread and soup, of course!

In the heat of the summer months, locals prefer to prepare salads instead of slaving for hours over a hot stove. In this chapter, you'll find such interesting recipes as: Basil-Tarragon Conch Salad; Shrimp, Grapefruit and Feta Salad, Caribbean Coleslaw and Cuban Black Bean, Rice and Pineapple Salad.

THE RECIPES

Marinated Conch Salad

Basil-Tarragon Conch Salad

Tuna and Papaya Salad

Shrimp, Grapefruit and Feta Salad

Lobster and Toasted Walnut Salad with Champagne Dressing

Scallop Salad with Caramelized Onions

Tomato, Orange and Lobster Salad with Toasted Pecans

Curried Chicken and Citrus Salad

Chicken and Avocado Salad with Orange-Scented Rice

Dilled Grapefruit and Broccoli Salad

Caribbean Coleslaw

Mango-Ginger Coleslaw

Garbanzo and Cilantro Salad

Cuban Black Bean, Rice and Pineapple Salad

Breadfruit Salad with Goat Cheese and Curried Mango Dressing

MARINATED CONCH SALAD

Region: The Keys

Conch salad is a staple in the Keys. Make this salad the night before and serve with crusty bread or crackers for a refreshing lunch. For those who prefer their food with a little added kick, substitute jalapeño or habañero pepper for the green bell pepper.

     2 pounds conch meat, cleaned
     2 large tomatoes, peeled, seeded and diced
     1 red bell pepper, finely chopped
     1 green bell pepper, finely chopped
     1 small yellow onion, finely chopped
     1 small stalk celery, diced
   1/2 cup Key lime or limejuice
     2 tablespoons cider vinegar
     2 tablespoons apple juice
     1 teaspoon Tabasco™
   1/2 teaspoon salt
   1/4 cup olive oil

1. Mince conch meat or run through food processor using a coarse blade.

2. Toss conch, along with tomatoes, bell peppers, onion, celery, lime juice, vinegar, apple juice, Tabasco™, salt and oil in a large non-reactive bowl (glass or ceramic only). Cover and marinate overnight in the refrigerator, at least eight hours, 12 is better. Serve on a bed of mixed greens.

BASIL-TARRAGON CONCH SALAD

Region: The Keys
Yield: about 6 servings

There are as many versions of conch salad as there are restaurants in the Florida and the Keys. This one is heart-healthy as it uses olive oil instead of mayonnaise. Try to use fresh herbs as the flavor is worth it.

     2 pounds conch, cleaned
   1/4 cup fresh Key lime or lime juice
     2 tablespoons cider vinegar
     1 small yellow onion, finely chopped
     1 clove garlic, crushed
     1 cucumber, peeled and diced
     1 large tomato, peeled, seeded and diced
     1 stalk celery, diced
   1/4 cup extra-virgin olive oil
   1/4 cup chopped fresh basil
     1 tablespoon chopped fresh tarragon or 1
        teaspoon dried
   1/2 cup chopped fresh chives
     1 teaspoon Tabasco™

1. Mince conch or run through a food processor or food mill. Transfer to a non-reactive bowl, cover and marinate overnight for at least eight hours in lime juice and vinegar.

2. Fold in onion, garlic, cucumber, tomato and celery. Set aside.

3. Whisk together olive oil, basil, tarragon, chives and Tabasco™ in a separate bowl.

4. Drizzle dressing over conch-vegetable mixture. Toss thoroughly and allow to marinate additional four hours.

TUNA AND PAPAYA SALAD

Region: Miami—Gold Coast
Yield: 4 to 6 servings

There's a world of flavor difference between fresh and tinned tuna. The next time grilled tuna is served for dinner, double the amount and use the extras for salad.

1 1/2 pounds broiled tuna, diced in bite-sized pieces
1 1/2 cups firm, yet ripe 1-inch papaya cubes
1/2 cup finely chopped green onions
1/4 cup finely chopped red onion
1 small jalapeño pepper, seeded and finely chopped (use only half for a milder flavor)
1 large stalk celery, diced
2 tablespoons Key lime or lime juice
1 tablespoon Tupelo honey (substitute regular honey)
3/4 cup mayonnaise
2 hard-cooked eggs, chopped
salt
fresh cracked black pepper

1. Toss tuna, papaya, green onions, red onion, jalapeño pepper and celery in a large bowl.

2. Combine lime juice, Tupelo honey and mayonnaise in a separate small bowl. Fold into tuna and papaya mixture.

3. Carefully cut in chopped eggs. Season to taste with salt and black pepper. Serve on a bed of lettuce or on bread as sandwiches.

DID YOU KNOW?

Walt Disney's Magic Kingdom in Orlando, Florida first opened October 1, 1971. Out of four theme parks, which include: Epcot, Disney-MGM Studios, and Disney's Animal Kingdom, the Magic Kingdom is the smallest at barely ninety-eight acres—yet it is still the most popular.

The entire park occupies 40-seven square miles, making it the largest theme park in the world.

2. Toss mayonnaise, Feta, Old Bay™ and oregano in a separate small bowl. Fold into shrimp mixture and set aside.

3. Season to taste with salt, pepper and cayenne, if desired.

LOBSTER AND TOASTED WALNUT SALAD WITH CHAMPAGNE DRESSING

Region: Central Florida, Citrus Country
Yield: 2 to 4 servings

Serve this rich salad on birthdays, anniversaries and other special occasions. Pink grapefruit gives it a tropical tang and combine nicely with the sweetness of the walnuts and bite of the green onions.

- 2 cups cooked diced lobster meat
- 1/2 cup chopped walnuts
- 1 1/2 cups chopped pink grapefruit sections
- 1/4 cup finely chopped green onions
- 3/4 cup chilled mayonnaise
- 1/4 cup chilled champagne
- 1 tablespoon Tupelo honey (substitute regular honey)
- 1/2 teaspoon cayenne pepper
- salt
- pepper

1. Pick over lobster meat for bones and cartilage. Place in refrigerator to chill.

SHRIMP, GRAPEFRUIT AND FETA SALAD

Region: Gulf Coast
Yield: 2 to 4 servings

- 2 cups coarsely diced cooked shrimp
- 2 cups grapefruit sections, seeded and coarsely chopped
- 3/4 cup mayonnaise
- 1/2 cup crumbled Feta cheese
- 1/2 teaspoon Old Bay™ seasoning
- 1 teaspoon dried oregano
- salt
- pepper
- cayenne pepper, if desired

1. Combine shrimp and grapefruit sections in a large bowl.

2. Arrange walnuts on a baking sheet and toast in a 350° oven for 10 minutes until lightly browned and fragrant. Do not burn. Remove from oven and set aside to cool.

3. Combine green onions, mayonnaise, chilled champagne, Tupelo honey and cayenne in a large bowl. Fold in lobster and grapefruit. Season to taste with salt and pepper.

SCALLOP SALAD WITH CARAMELIZED ONIONS

Region: Northeast
Yield: 4 servings

To caramelize a vegetable means to change the carbon content of the sugar by long heat times. Instead of just sautéing onions for most recipes, I'll take the time to get the exquisite caramelized flavor.

1 1/2 pounds scallops
1 cup water
2 tablespoons cider vinegar
2 tablespoons olive oil
1 large yellow onion, finely chopped
1 clove garlic, crushed
1 stalk celery, diced
1/4 cup sweet pickle relish
1/4 cup chopped fresh parsley
1 cup mayonnaise
salt
pepper

1. Boil scallops in the 1-cup water water in a medium saucepan for 10 minutes. Drain, cool, dice and toss with vinegar. Chill uncovered in the refrigerator.

2. Sauté onions in the olive oil over medium-high heat, stirring constantly until onions are beginning to brown, about 20 minutes. Lower heat and keep cooking, stirring constantly, until onions are a luscious dark brown color, another five to six minutes. Remove from heat, cool and set aside.

3. Combine garlic, celery, sweet pickle relish, parsley and mayonnaise in a large bowl. Fold in chilled scallops and cooled onions. Season to taste with salt and pepper. Serve on a bed of lettuce, with crusty bread and chilled white wine. Serve on a bed of mixed greens.

DID YOU KNOW?

Fort Lauderdale's nickname is 'Venice of America' because of its 300 miles of boat-friendly, canal-laced waterways.

TOMATO, ORANGE AND LOBSTER SALAD WITH TOASTED PECANS

Region: Central Florida, Citrus Country
Yield: 4 servings

Substitute shrimp, crab or any firm, cooked and chilled white fish for the lobster.

1	pound cooked lobster, diced and chilled
1 1/2	cup chopped pecans
4	cups mesculun or other baby lettuce greens
4	medium, ripe tomatoes
1	pound cooked lobster meat, chilled
1/4	cup orange juice
2	oranges, peeled, sectioned and chopped
1/4	cup balsamic vinegar
1/2	cup extra-virgin olive oil
1	tablespoon dried Italian seasoning
1/2	teaspoon salt
1/2	teaspoon fresh cracked black pepper
1/8	teaspoon ground cinnamon

1. Toast pecans on an ungreased cookie sheet in a 400º oven until golden. Set aside.

2. Divide greens among four dinner plates. Using a sharp knife, slice tomatoes thinly and arrange evenly over lettuce. Top with chilled lobster, dividing equally between the plates.

3. Combine orange juice, orange sections, vinegar, olive oil, Italian seasoning, salt, black pepper and cinnamon in a non-reactive small bowl.

4. Drizzle over salad. Top with toasted pecans.

CURRIED CHICKEN AND CITRUS SALAD

Region: Florida—Caribbean
Yield: 4 to 6 servings

1/2	cup fresh diced pineapple
1	small orange, peeled, sectioned, seeded and chopped
1/2	white or pink grapefruit, peeled, sectioned, seeded and chopped
2	teaspoons curry powder
2	tablespoons mayonnaise
1	small red onion, finely chopped
1	garlic clove, crushed
2	cups diced cooked chicken meat
1/4	cup raisins
4	cups salad greens (spinach, mesculun or romaine)

1. Place pineapple, orange and grapefruit in a colander set over a bowl. Reserve any drained juice and use for tropical drinks.

2. Toast curry powder in a small, dry skillet over moderate heat for one minute to eliminate raw taste of spices. Remove from heat and cool for five minutes.

3. Combine mayonnaise, curry powder, onion and garlic in a medium bowl. Fold in chicken and raisins to coat. Chill covered in the refrigerator for two hours.

4. Divide greens between four to six plates. Arrange a scoop of chicken salad over lettuce.

CHICKEN AND AVOCADO SALAD WITH ORANGE-SCENTED RICE

Region: Central Florida, Citrus Country
Yield: 4 to 6 servings

Basmati rice, with the addition of orange rind, adds an exotic Eastern touch to this salad.

1 cup water
1 cup canned low-sodium chicken broth
1 tablespoon grated fresh orange rind
1 large orange, peeled, sectioned, seeded and chopped
1 cup basmati rice (white or brown)
2 cups cooked diced chicken

1 stalk celery, finely chopped
1/4 cup finely chopped red onion
1 garlic clove, crushed
juice of 1 large orange (4 tablespoons)
juice of 1 lemon (3 tablespoons)
1 tablespoon cider vinegar
1 tablespoon Tupelo honey (substitute regular honey)
1/4 cup olive oil
1 teaspoon fresh cracked black pepper
1 teaspoon dried Italian herbs
4 cups salad greens
1 avocado (do not cut until read to serve salad)

1. Heat water and chicken broth to boiling in a medium saucepan. Add orange rind (reserve chopped orange) and rice to boiling broth, returning to a boil. Reduce heat to simmer, cover and cook until all water has been absorbed, about 20 to 40 minutes depending upon type of rice. Remove from heat; turn out into a large, heat-proof bowl to cool completely.

2. Fold in cooled rice, orange sections, chicken, celery, onion and garlic. Set aside. Combine orange juice, lemon juice, vinegar, Tupelo honey, pepper and herbs in a small bowl. Drizzle over chicken rice mixture, tossing well. Chill uncovered for two hours in refrigerator.

3. Serve on a bed of greens, along with pita bread wedges or crusty bread. Peel avocado, slice thinly and arrange over salad.

DILLED GRAPEFRUIT AND BROCCOLI SALAD

Region: Central Florida, Citrus Country
Yield: 4 to 6 servings

2 medium pink grapefruits, peeled and sectioned
1/4 cup olive oil
2 tablespoons finely chopped red onion
1 garlic clove, crushed
3 tablespoons cider vinegar
2 tablespoons chopped fresh dill
1 tablespoon Dijon-style mustard
1 teaspoon dried Italian herbs
3 cups broccoli florets, lightly steamed for seven minutes, then chilled

1. Chop grapefruit sections into bite-size pieces, removing any seeds. Place in strainer over a bowl to drain, reserving juice.

2. Combine olive oil, onion, garlic, vinegar, dill and mustard. Stir in Italian herbs and any drained grapefruit juice.

3. Toss broccoli and grapefruit with dressing. Cover and marinate at least two hours in refrigerator.

CARIBBEAN COLESLAW

Region: Florida—Caribbean
Yield: about 6 servings

3 cups shredded green cabbage (1 small head)
3 cups shredded red cabbage (1 small head)
1 cup grated carrot
1/4 cup raisins
2 large oranges, peeled, sectioned and diced
3/4 cup mayonnaise
1/4 cup Key lime or lime juice
1/2 teaspoon curry powder, toasted in a dry skillet for 1 minute
salt
pepper

1. Toss together green and red cabbage with carrot in a large non-reactive bowl. Fold in raisins and oranges. Set aside.

2. Mix mayonnaise with lime juice and curry powder. Fold into cabbage mixture. Season to taste with salt and pepper.

MANGO-GINGER COLESLAW

Region: Florida—Caribbean
Yield: 6 servings

Fresh ginger has a much more pungent flavor than dried, which is a lackluster substitute. High in potassium, ginger has antiseptic properties, assists with fevers, reduces over eager appetites, and helps with indigestion and motion sickness.

- 6 cups shredded green cabbage (1 medium to large head)
- 1 cup shredded carrot
- 2 cups fresh diced mango
- 3/4 cup mayonnaise
- 1 teaspoon packed brown sugar
- 1 teaspoon Dijon-style mustard
- 1 tablespoon grated fresh ginger
- 2 tablespoons capers
- salt
- pepper

1. Toss cabbage, carrot and mango in a large, non-reactive bowl. Set aside.

2. Combine mayonnaise, brown sugar, mustard and ginger in a small bowl. Fold into cabbage mixture. Gently mix in capers.

3. Season to taste with salt and pepper.

GARBANZO AND CILANTRO SALAD

Region: Florida—Caribbean
Yield: 4 servings

I have an apartment in San Juan, Puerto Rico. An herb called culantro (imagine the freshness and flavor of cilantro multiplied by ten!) is readily available on the island. The scent of culantro is so strong that it will permeate the entire refrigerator. So, if you can find it, substitute culantro for the cilantro. Culantro can be easily grown from seed like any other herb.

- 2 cups cooked or canned garbanzo beans, drained and rinsed
- 1 medium yellow onion, finely chopped
- 2 garlic cloves, crushed
- 1/4 cup Key lime juice
- 1/4 cup olive oil
- 1/4 cup chopped fresh cilantro
- 1/2 teaspoon dried oregano
- 1/2 teaspoon dried thyme
- salt
- pepper

1. Combine garbanzos, onion and garlic in a large, non-reactive bowl. Set aside.

2. Stir together lime juice, olive oil, cilantro, oregano and thyme in a cup

or small bowl. Drizzle over garbanzo mixture. Season to taste with salt and pepper. Toss to combine.

CUBAN BLACK BEAN, RICE AND PINEAPPLE SALAD

Region: Miami—Cuban
Yield: 6 servings

Chilled black beans and rice make for a refreshing salad on sultry summer days. Pineapple adds sweetness, the hot peppers a touch of fire.

 2 cups cooked black beans, or equivalent in canned (rinsed and drained)
 2 cups cooked rice
 1 cup fresh diced pineapple
 1/4 cup chopped fresh green onions
 1/4 cup chopped fresh chives
 2 garlic cloves, crushed
 1/4 cup chopped, pimento-stuffed green olives
 1/4 cup chopped fresh cilantro
 1/2 teaspoon ground cumin
 1/2 teaspoon dried oregano
 1 small jalapeño pepper, seeded and finely chopped
 1/2 cup olive oil
 1/4 cup fresh Key Lime or lime juice
 salt
 pepper

1. Combine beans, rice, pineapple, green onions, chives, garlic, olives, cilantro, cumin, oregano and jalapeño peppers in a large, non-reactive bowl. Set aside.

2. Combine olive oil and lime juice, drizzling over salad. Toss gently. Season to taste to salt and pepper.

NOTE: Fresh pineapple is preferred, but canned makes a decent substitution.

BREADFRUIT SALAD WITH GOAT CHEESE AND CURRIED MANGO DRESSING

Region: Central Florida
Yield: 6 servings

Breadfruit is a tree native to the East Indian Ocean and Pacific Ocean islands. Captain Bligh, who sailed all over the world to find breadfruit, introduced it to the Caribbean islands on the HMS Bounty in the late 18th century to be used as an inexpensive food source for the slaves used to work the sugar plantations. And then they didn't want to eat it!
I've combined this starchy, potato-like fruit with my two favorite flavors—curry and mango. Mango is high in beta-carotene, which is wonderful for your skin and general health, and the turmeric in curry is a mild anti-inflammatory.

1 breadfruit (about 3 pounds), boiled, peeled and cut in 1-inch cubes
1 large onion, finely chopped
2 teaspoons (more or less to taste) curry powder
1 cup fresh or frozen mango chunks
1/4 cup cider vinegar
1/4 cup extra-virgin olive oil
4 ounces goat cheese, crumbled
salt
pepper

1. Toss breadfruit and onion in a large, non-reactive bowl. Set aside.

2. Toast curry powder for one minute over medium heat in a medium skillet. Remove from heat and fold in mango, vinegar and olive oil.

3. Puree mango mixture in a food processor or blender.

4. Spoon goat cheese over breadfruit. Fold in mango mixture, tossing gently. Season to taste with salt and pepper.

NOTE: You can substitute boiled red, waxy potatoes for the breadfruit.

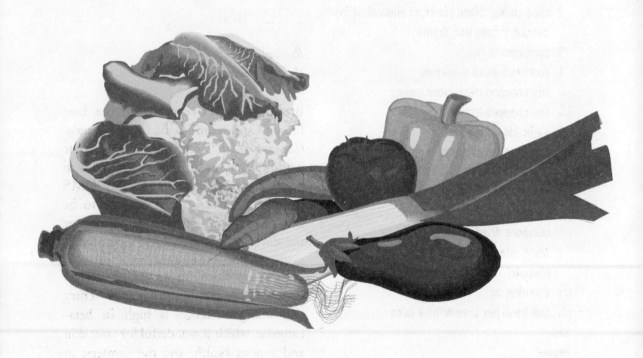

Equatorial Vegetables and Sides

VEGETABLES AND SIDE DISHES are ordinarily served to round out and compliment a meal. Some, like soups and salads, can be served as meals on their own,

Consider serving *Cuban Black Beans and Rice* together with *Garlicky Plaintain* and *Hush Puppies*. *Orange, Tomato and Mozarella Tower* combines nicely with soup and salad for a ladies luncheon.

A number of the sides in this chapter are naturally sweet. *Carmalized Plaintain, Rum-Baked Yams and Oranges,* and *Cinnamon-Coconut Sweet Potatoes* make a perfect foil for the Caribbean-inspired curries in this book and other fiery dishes.

Try any combination of these unusual side dishes to enliven your menus.

THE RECIPES

Swamp Cabbage (Hearts of Palm)

Orange, Tomato and Mozzarella Tower

Spicy Fried Cabbage with Raisins

Cuban Black Beans and Rice

Pigeon Peas and Rice

Yellow Rice

Green Bananas with Bacon, Onions and Peppers

Garlicky Plantain

Caramelized Plantain

Rum-Baked Yams and Oranges

Cinnamon-Coconut Sweet Potatoes

Fried Green Tomatoes in Garlic Sauce

Hush Puppies

Southern Cornbread

SWAMP CABBAGE (HEARTS OF PALM)

Region: The Everglades
Yield: 4 servings

In Florida's history, each time a palm was chopped down to make room for a new home or road, hearts of palm became available to the early settlers of the Florida peninsula. Serve with my favorite, fresh hot cornbread.

    4   swamp cabbages (6 by 2 inches), or 2
        14-ounce cans hearts of palm
    2   ounces salt pork or bacon
  3/4   cup water
    3   tablespoons cider vinegar
  hot pepper sauce
  salt
  pepper

1. Dice swamp cabbage into bite-size pieces. Combine swamp cabbage with salt pork and water in a medium saucepan. Bring to boil, reduce heat, cover and simmer for 25 minutes until tender, yet still crunchy.

2. Remove from heat, and sprinkle with vinegar. Toss to combine. Season to taste with hot pepper sauce, salt and pepper.

ORANGE, TOMATO AND MOZZARELLA TOWER

Region: Central Florida, Citrus Country
Yield: 4 servings

The addition of juicy oranges adds a refreshing twist to this classic.

    2   medium oranges
    8   medium size lettuce leaves
   12   1/4-inch thick mozzarella slices
    2   medium ripe tomatoes, thinly sliced
   12   basil leaves
  1/4   cup orange juice
  juice of one lemon
    2   tablespoons balsamic vinegar
  1/4   cup olive oil
    1   teaspoon dried Italian herbs
  1/2   teaspoon sea salt
  1/2   teaspoon fresh cracked black pepper

1. Peel orange and thinly slice. Place slices on a cookie sheet beneath the broiler for five to eight minutes until lightly seared. Remove from heat and cool.

2. Arrange two lettuce leaves on each plate. Place mozzarella slice on each plate over lettuce. Follow with tomato slice and basil leaf. Continue layering with mozzarella slice, then orange slice and so forth. Secure with toothpicks and set aside.

3. Combine orange juice, lemon juice, vinegar, olive oil, herbs, salt and black pepper in a small bowl.

4. Drizzle over towers. Chill uncovered in the refrigerator for two hours.

....

SPICY FRIED CABBAGE WITH RAISINS

Region: Central Florida
Yield: 6 to 8 servings

Go easy on the red pepper flakes, adding small amounts at a time and tasting before adding more. Even a quarter teaspoon of red pepper flakes can blow your tonsils out. The raisins offset the fire a tad.

8 strips of bacon
1/2 teaspoon ground cumin
6 cups shredded green cabbage (1 medium head)
1 large carrot, shredded
1/2 cup raisins
1/4 teaspoon red pepper flakes
salt
pepper

1. Fry bacon over medium-high heat in a large skillet until crisp. Drain off fat, reserving about 2 tablespoons in skillet. Drain bacon on food-grade paper towels. Set aside.

2. Add cumin to skillet and fry for one minute until slightly darkened.

3. Toss in cabbage, carrot, raisins and red pepper flakes to skillet. Sauté or

---

CABBAGE

Cabbage is a cruciferous vegetable belonging to the same family as broccoli, kale, cauliflower, kohlrabi and Brussels sprouts. Around 600 B.C. cabbage traveled to Europe via Asia Minor. There are over 400 varieties of cabbage.

Purchasing: Choose a cabbage heavy for its size. Check the outside leaves for black mold marks. Easier done on a light cabbage than a dark cabbage. Should be free of cracks.

Preparation: Remove outer leaves. Soak in salt or vinegar water for 20 minutes. Rinse well.

Cooking: Do not over cook. Like most overdone vegetables essential nutrients are lost and much of the flavor.

Storing: Cabbage can be kept for weeks in a refrigerated drawer of your refrigerator. I have to admit I've kept cabbage weeks longer than that. Just peel off the outside leaves.

Nutritional info: Vitamin C, folic acid, potassium, some Vitamin B6. Good for stomach ulcers, and said to have cancer inhibiting properties.

seven to eight minutes, until cabbage is wilted but slightly crunchy. Crumble reserved bacon over top and toss. Season to taste with salt and black pepper.

NOTE: You can omit the bacon and substitute 2 tablespoons of olive oil instead. You may need to add an extra dash of salt to make up for the bacon's saltiness.

CUBAN BLACK BEANS AND RICE

Region: Miami—Cuban
Yield: about 4 servings

Toasting the cumin and coriander in a dry skillet takes away the raw taste from the spices, and adds a deep, smoky complexity to this Cuban recipe.

  2 cups dried black beans, soaked overnight and drained
  6 cups water
  1 teaspoon ground cumin
1/2 teaspoon ground coriander
1/4 pound bacon or salt pork, diced
  1 large onion, finely chopped
  4 cloves garlic, crushed
  2 bay leaves
  1 teaspoon dried thyme
salt
pepper
  1 medium yellow onion finely chopped

1. Bring the 6 cups of water to a boil in a deep kettle. Rinse pre-soaked beans and add to kettle. Return to boil, reduce heat, cover and simmer for one and a half hours.

2. Toast cumin and coriander in a large skillet over medium heat for one to two minutes until lightly browned and a fragrant aroma is emitted. Add bacon or salt pork to skillet and fry, stirring constantly for two minutes.

3. Sauté onion and garlic in the bacon fat until onion is soft and bits are browned. Drain off all but a couple tablespoons of the oil.

4. Scrape remaining onion-bacon mixture into kettle with black beans. Add bay leaves and thyme. Return to boil, reduce heat, cover and simmer for 30 minutes.

5. Remove from heat and discard bay leaves. Season to taste with salt and pepper. Ladle into individual serving bowls and top with a generous spoonful of finely chopped onion.

PIGEON PEAS AND RICE

Region: Florida—Caribbean
Yield: 4 servings

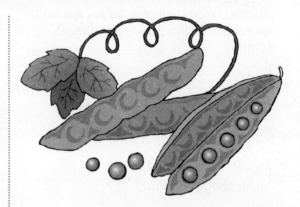

Pigeon pea recipes abound all over the Caribbean, including Puerto Rico and the Virgin Islands. My daughter's grandmother serves this up when the grandchildren come to visit. Pigeon peas can be found in the canned or frozen section of your grocer. Use long-grain rice for this dish as it cooks up fluffier than medium or short grain.

- 2 tablespoons olive oil
- 1 medium yellow onion, finely chopped
- 4 large garlic cloves, crushed
- 1/2 teaspoon dried thyme
- 1/2 small jalapeño or habañero pepper, carefully seeded and finely chopped
- 1/2 small red bell pepper, finely chopped
- 1/2 small can tomato paste
- 1 cup uncooked long-grain rice
- 2 cups water
- 1 (14.5-ounce) can pigeon peas, drained and rinsed
- salt
- pepper

1. Sauté the onion and garlic in the olive oil in a medium skillet over moderate heat until translucent, four or five minutes. Stir in thyme and jalapeño pepper. Cook until onions are lightly browned, another four minutes or so. Add bell pepper, and cook another two minutes.

2. Whisk in tomato paste, rice and water. Bring to a boil, reduce heat, simmer and cover for fifteen minutes until rice is cooked.

3. Fold in pigeon peas and continue cooking uncovered, but stirring occasionally. Season to taste with salt and pepper.

YELLOW RICE

Region: Miami—Cuban
Yield: 4 servings

Annatto, also known as achiote seed, is available both whole and ground. Used in both Indian and Hispanic cuisine for its earthy, iodine-like flavor and color. It is also used to give butter and cheese its deep yellow color, which I didn't know myself until recently. Hey, at least its not artificial color.

- 2 tablespoons olive oil
- 1 teaspoon annatto
- 1 medium onion, finely chopped
- 2 large cloves garlic, crushed
- 1 teaspoon sea salt
- 1 cup long-grain rice
- 2 cups water
- 1/4 cup finely chopped cilantro or culantro (see index) leaves
- pepper

1. Heat the olive oil and annatto over moderate heat in a saucepan large enough to cook rice. Oil should turn a bright red after a couple of minutes. Strain and discard annatto seed.

2. Sauté onion and garlic in the annatto oil over medium-high heat until onion is soft and lightly browned, about six or seven minutes.

3. Fold in salt and rice, cooking over medium heat, stirring so rice is completely coated with oil for two to three minutes.

4. Add water and cilantro, bring to boil, reduce heat, cover and simmer until all water is absorbed. Season to taste with pepper and additional salt if needed.

GREEN BANANAS WITH BACON, ONIONS AND PEPPERS

Region: Miami—Cuban
Yield: about 6 servings

Having lived in the Caribbean most of my life, I have never particularly cared for boiled, unripe bananas, until I came across this recipe in a Cuban restaurant in Little Havana (between Doral and Miami). My daughter Roxanne and I got lost there when we first moved to Florida.

- 4 green bananas
- 2 slices bacon or a 2-by-2-inch chunk of salt pork
- 1 medium onion, finely chopped
- 1 green bell pepper, finely chopped
- 2 cloves garlic, crushed
- 1/2 teaspoon Tabasco™
- salt
- cayenne pepper

1. Fill a large pot with salted water and bring to a boil.

2. Peel green bananas and cut in half, or if particularly large, in thirds. Carefully lower bananas into boiling water, avoiding splashes.

3. Cook for five minutes. Remove with a slotted spoon and drain on clean kitchen towels.

4. Fry bacon in a large skillet until crunchy. Remove bacon, drain on food-grade paper towels and reserve. Drain off all but 2 tablespoons of the fat and sauté onions, garlic and bell peppers for six or seven minutes until lightly browned over medium heat. Stir in Tabasco™.

5. Slice bananas in 1-inch wheels. Fold into onion mixture in skillet. Crumble bacon over top. Toss lightly and remove from heat. Sprinkle with salt and cayenne pepper to taste.

GARLICKY PLANTAIN

Region: Miami—Cuban
Yield: 6 servings

Plantains belong to the banana family. Unlike bananas, they cannot be eaten raw. Select plantains that are turning black with flecks of yellow. This is when they are actually ripe! If you're a fan of bananas, you'll enjoy sautéed plantain as a sweet foil to spicy bean dishes, chicken, pork or fish.

  3 large ripe plantains
  4 tablespoons butter
  2 garlic cloves, crushed
salt
pepper

1. Peel plantain with a sharp knife like a banana. Slice in 1/2 inch slices on the diagonal.

2. Heat 2 tablespoons of the butter in a large skillet over moderate heat.

3. Add plantain slices and garlic to skillet and cook for 10 minutes on one side over medium heat. Flip plantain slices; add remaining butter and sauté for additional seven to eight minutes until light golden brown.

4. Drain on food-grade white paper towels. Season to taste with salt and pepper.

CARAMELIZED PLANTAIN

*Region: Panhandle, Tallahassee
to Pensacola*
Yield: 6 servings

If you're a fan of Banana's Foster, you'll enjoy this dish. Serve as a side dish or as a dessert with a scoop of vanilla ice cream. Be generous with the cinnamon—it's a known blood sugar stabilizer.

3 ripe plantains (see previous recipe)
1 teaspoon cinnamon
1/4 teaspoon ground cardamom
2 tablespoons packed brown sugar
4 tablespoons butter

1. Peel plantains like a banana and slice in 1/2 -inch slices on the diagonal.

2. Dry roast the cinnamon and cardamom in a large skillet over moderate heat for one minute until lightly toasted and fragrant aroma is released.

3. Add brown sugar, butter and plantain slices, reduce heat and cook for 15 to 20 minutes until plantain is lightly browned (flipping once).

4. Serve while hot.

RUM-BAKED YAMS AND ORANGES

Region: Central Florida, Citrus Country
Yield: 4 servings

When I was a child, our family drove to Florida from Massachusetts every year to vacation. I still recall the bags of sweet-tart oranges and spicy orange blossom perfume with which my parents returned to Massachusetts. Our treasures from Florida were divided among friends and family. The combination of yams and oranges in this recipe is heady.

4 medium yams, scrubbed
4 large oranges
1/4 cup (1/2 stick) butter
1/4 cup dark rum
1/4 teaspoon ground cardamom

1. Preheat oven to 400°. Bake yams for 45 minutes until soft. Remove from oven and set aside until cool enough to handle.

2. Carefully wash the outside of the oranges (I use an organic fruit and vegetable wash). Slice off tops of oranges (reserve tops for rind), and using a serrated spoon, scoop out orange pulp.

3. Using a citrus juicer, juice the pulp, removing and seeds and reserve the juice.

IS THERE A DIFFERENCE BETWEEN YAMS AND SWEET POTATOES?

Yes and no. Several decades ago, when orange-fleshed sweet potatoes arrived in the U.S. shippers wanted to distinguish between this orange potato and ordinary white potatoes. Therefore, yams are really sweet potatoes with orange flesh.

4. Grate orange tops until they yield 1 tablespoon of orange peel. Set aside.

5. Peel yams and transfer to a large bowl. Mash with butter, rum, cardamom, orange juice and orange rind.

6. Transfer mashed yams to hollowed out orange shells. Bake in 350° oven for 20 minutes.

CINNAMON AND COCONUT SWEET POTATOES

Region: Central Florida
Yield: 4 to 6 servings

I was introduced to cinnamon and coconut in Puerto Rico, where the combination is served as a delicious candy. Sweet potatoes are a tropical tuber, which grows prolifically in Florida. This recipe is totally tropical and good for you. High in Vitamin A, good source of potassium. Also contains some Vitamin C, Vitamin B6, copper, pantothenic acid and folic acid.

3 pounds sweet potatoes, scrubbed
1/4 cup (1/2 stick) butter
1 teaspoon cinnamon
1 tablespoon packed brown sugar, preferably dark
1/2 teaspoon grated fresh lemon rind
1/4 teaspoon ground cardamom
1/2 teaspoon salt
1/4 cup grated fresh coconut, or packaged unsweetened shredded

1. Preheat oven to 400°. Bake sweet potatoes for 45 minutes or until soft. Remove from oven until cool enough to handle.

2. Peel sweet potatoes and transfer pulp to a large saucepan. Mash lightly.

3. Add butter, cinnamon, sugar, lemon rind, cardamom and salt. Simmer over low heat for five minutes, stirring occasionally.

4. Fold in coconut and remove from heat. Serve while hot.

FRIED GREEN TOMATOES IN GARLIC SAUCE

Region: Lake Okeechobee
Yield: about 4 servings

If you've never had fried green tomatoes, you're in for a treat.

```
 6  tablespoons flour
 1  teaspoon dried Italian seasoning
1/2 teaspoon fresh cracked black pepper
 2  eggs
 4 to 6 large green tomatoes, thinly sliced
oil for frying
1/4 cup olive oil
 4  garlic cloves, crushed
1/2 teaspoon salt
```

1. Combine flour, Italian seasoning and black pepper in a small bowl. Beat eggs lightly in a separate bowl.

2. Heat 1/4-inch of oil in a large skillet to 350º.

3. Dip tomato slices in eggs, then roll in flour mixture. Shake off excess. Fry tomatoes until golden on each side.

4. Line a cookie sheet with food-grade paper towels and keep tomato slices warm in oven.

5. Heat olive oil and garlic in a small skillet until garlic is golden. Stir in salt. Serve as a dipping sauce with fried tomato.

DID YOU KNOW?

The Everglades are nearly twice the size of Delaware. Created in 1947, this national park encompasses some 4,000 square miles. The Everglades are the only subtropical park in North America. El Yunque in Puerto Rico is the only tropical rainforest in the National Park System.

The unique ecosystem of the park works in several ways: the swamp areas have vegetation, which filters water traveling through its streams; it holds down flooding to outlying areas after torrential rains; and serves as a habitat for many animals and potentially endangered plant life.

HUSH PUPPIES

Region: Panhandle, Deep South
Yield: about 18

The addition of corn kernels adds a nice, chewy texture to the hush puppies.

1 1/2 cups cornmeal
1/2 cup all-purpose flour
1/2 teaspoon baking soda
1 teaspoon salt
1/8 teaspoon ground cardamom
1 egg, lightly beaten
1 cup buttermilk
1/2 cup corn kernels, fresh or frozen
vegetable oil for frying

1. Combine cornmeal, flour, baking soda, salt and cardamom in a medium bowl. Set aside.

2. Combine egg and buttermilk in a separate small bowl.

3. Gradually stir butter milk mixture into dry ingredients. Fold in corn kernels.

4. Heat 1-inch of oil in a deep heavy skillet to 350°. Drop batter by spoonfuls into hot fat. Fry until golden. Drain on food-grade white paper towels.

SOUTHERN CORNBREAD

Region: Florida Panhandle, Deep South
Yield: 6 to 8 servings

Most of us are used to a sweet, cakey cornbread, sort of like the kind served at public school lunches. I asked my daughter, who attended private school, and she said the cornbread was about the same at her school, like a saccharine lump of clay. Traditionally Southern-style cornbread is just the opposite: thin, crusty and savory. There is no sugar in Southern cornbread, but I have taken the liberty of adding a mere 2 teaspoons to this recipe. Sugar adds texture to baked goods. This recipe came to me via my neighbor's 92-year-old grandmother, who in turn received it from her grandmother.

3/4 cup yellow or white cornmeal
1/4 cup all-purpose flour
2 teaspoons sugar
2 teaspoons baking powder
1/2 teaspoon salt
1/4 teaspoon baking soda
1/3 cup boiling water
1/2 cup buttermilk
1/4 cup whole milk
1 large egg, lightly beaten
4 teaspoons bacon drippings, or 2 tea spoons vegetable oil combined with 2 teaspoons melted butter
1/2 cup corn kernels, or drained, canned

1. Preheat oven to 400º F. Grease an 8-inch square baking dish.

2. Place half of the cornmeal (about a 1/3 cup) in a small bowl. Combine remaining cornmeal, flour, sugar, baking powder, salt and baking soda in another bowl.

3. Pour rapidly boiling water over the first third cup of the cornmeal, beating until smooth and stiff.

Drizzle in buttermilk, whole milk and egg.

4. Quickly stir remaining dry ingredients into wet ingredients until combined. Whisk in bacon fat or vegetable oil-butter combination. Fold in corn kernels. Pour batter into prepared pan. Bake until golden, about 25 to 30 minutes. A toothpick inserted in center should come out clean.

Caribbean Sandwiches

TIME IS SHORT. Few of us have much spare time for cooking. Well, except for maybe me, and it's my job to cook! There's no reason not to eat well, and savor a few minutes respite from work, family and daily anxieties. Cuban Roast Pork Sandwiches, Garlicky Fried Fish Sandwiches and Conch Burgers fit the bill for exceptional taste and swift preparation time.

THE RECIPES

CUBAN BREAD

Region: Miami—Cuban
Yield: 2 loaves

No sandwich is complete without bread, so why not homemade? And why not Cuban? Cuban bread resembles French bread, just lighter and crustier. Although it is made with the same ingredients, the process is different. The dough is placed in an unheated oven, allowed to sit for a few minutes, then, when the oven is turned on, begins to rise. The end result is a very thin and crispy crust because the bread continues to rise. The nice part about this recipe is that it's fat-free. But, that also means it spoils quickly. Best if used in 24 hours.

- 2 packages dry yeast
- 2 cups warm water (105° to 115° F)
- 1 teaspoon sugar
- 1/2 teaspoon Tupelo honey
- 1 1/2 teaspoons salt
- 1 tablespoon, plus 1 teaspoon granulated, white sugar
- 5+ cups of flour (you may need up to another cup of flour depending upon the moisture content of your flour)
- 1 tablespoon vegetable oil
- 3/4 cup coarse cornmeal

1. Dissolve yeast in a large bowl in warm water, along with sugar, honey and salt. Allow to sit for 10 minutes.

2. Gradually cut in 3 cups of the flour into the yeast using a dough hook or wooden spatula. Beat vigorously for two minutes. Slowly add sugar and remaining flour until dough forms a mass and begins to pull away from the sides of the bowl.

3. Turn the dough onto a floured board. Knead for about 10 minutes until you have a smooth, elastic dough. Blisters will form on the surface. Wet hands with a tablespoon of vegetable oil and coat surface of dough ball evenly.

4. Place in a bowl and cover with a clean towel. Keep in a warm place until doubled in size, about an hour and a half.

5. Punch down dough, and knead for five minutes, then form into two balls. Flatten ball slightly to about three inches high.

6. Sprinkle a cookie sheet with the cornmeal and place dough on top. Score top of loaf diagonally with a knife and brush with cold water.

7. Place loaves in cold oven. Wait 10 minutes. Then add a pan of hot water to oven to steam bread. Set oven for 400°. Bake for 40 minutes until golden.

CUBAN ROAST PORK SANDWICHES

Region: Miami—Cuban
Yield: 4 large sandwiches

It's important to remember that Cuban sandwiches are not a mélange of leftover deli meats, such as turkey or roast beef. Traditionally these Cuban sandwiches are pressed between the irons of a hot sandwich press. The bread becomes golden and crunchy on the outside, flattened and the cheese, gooey and melted.

- 1 loaf homemade Cuban bread or French bread
- 3 tablespoons Dijon-style mustard
- 1 tablespoon light, gold or dark rum
- 1/4 pound roast pork, thinly sliced
- 1/4 pound ham
- 1/4 pound Genoa salami
- 1/2 pound Swiss cheese
  sliced sour or dill pickles
  butter or pork drippings

1. Cut loaf of bread in four pieces, then slice each in half. Combine mustard and rum in a small bowl, and spread over sandwich halves.

2. Divide ham, salami, pork and cheese evenly between four sandwiches. Add a row of pickles, then top with remaining bread.

3. Using the sandwich grill, heat the bread through, about four minutes, until cheese melts. If you don't have a grill, wrap sandwiches in foil and bake in a 375° degree oven for 10 minutes.

GARLICKY FRIED FISH SANDWICH

Region: The Keys
Yield: 2 sandwiches

Use fresh herbs if available to season the bread crumbs. I purchased a hand-crank herb mill to make short work of chopping the herbs. If using dried herbs, reduce recipe quantity by two-thirds.

- 1/4 cup plain bread crumbs
- 2 teaspoons chopped fresh parsley
- 1 teaspoon chopped fresh basil
- 1 teaspoon chopped fresh oregano
- 1/2 teaspoon chopped fresh thyme
- 1/2 teaspoon chopped fresh rosemary
- 1 large clove garlic, crushed
  vegetable oil for frying
- 1/2 pound dolphin, mahi-mahi or grouper fillets
- 1 egg, lightly beaten
- 2 tablespoons whole milk
- 1/4 cup all-purpose flour
- 1 tablespoon olive oil
- 1 tablespoon butter
- 1/2 small onion, sliced in rings
- 2 slices sharp Cheddar or American cheese
- 4 slices good-quality white or whole wheat bread

tomato slices

lettuce leaves

tartar sauce

1. Combine bread crumbs, parsley, basil, oregano, thyme, rosemary and garlic in a small bowl. Set aside.

2. Heat 1/4 inch of oil to 350° in a large, heavy skillet.

3. Whisk together egg and milk in a small bowl. Dip dolphin fillets in egg mixture and then flour. Shake off excess flour. Dip in egg again, then in bread crumb mixture.

4. Fry fish until golden on each side. Drain on food-grade white paper towels. Place in warm oven.

5. Heat olive oil and butter in a small skillet. Sauté onion rings until golden and sweet. Set aside.

6. Toast bread. Place slices of cheese on two slices of the toast. Broil in oven until melted.

7. Top remaining two slices of toast with fish fillets, arranging onion rings over top. Divide lettuce and tomato evenly between two sandwiches. Spoon tartar sauce as desired, top with remaining slices of cheese toast.

HEMINGWAY'S SPECIAL

Region: The Keys
Yield: 2 sandwiches

Ernest Hemingway arrived in Key West in 1928 thanks to fellow writer John dos Passos. Hemingway rented a house with his second wife, Pauline, spending winters in the Keys, and summers in Europe and Wyoming. In 1931, Pauline's uncle gave the couple a house at 907 Whitehead Street, today preserved as Hemingway Home and Museum.

  1 tablespoon olive oil

1/2 small onion, thinly sliced in rings

1/2 cup green bell pepper slices

  1 large clove garlic, crushed

1/2 cup sliced mushrooms

  1 egg, lightly beaten

  2 tablespoons evaporated milk (unsweetened)

vegetable oil for frying

1/2 cup seasoned bread crumbs

1/2 pound grouper, mahi-mahi or dolphin fillets

  2 bulky rolls or sesame rolls

  2 slices yellow cheese (choose a sharp cheese such as Cheddar or a mild American)

lettuce

tomato slices

1. Sauté onions, bell peppers, garlic and mushrooms in the olive oil in a medium skillet over moderate heat until onions are golden, about six minutes. Set aside.

2. Whisk together egg and evaporated milk on a small plate with a lip. Place breadcrumbs on another plate.

3. Heat 1/4 inch of the vegetable oil in a large, heavy skillet until 350°.

4. Dip the fish fillets in egg mixture, then in the bread crumbs. Shake off excess, then fry until golden. Drain on food-grade white paper towels. Reserve in warm oven.

5. Slice rolls in half and top two halves with the two slices of cheese. Broil in oven until cheese melts.

6. Top two halves with grouper fillets. Garnish with lettuce and tomato, then onion-mushroom mixture. Top with melted cheese buns.

DUVAL STREET CONCH BURGER

Region: The Keys
Yield: 4 conch burgers

1 1/4 cups boiled conch meat, run through a food processor
1 cup seasoned bread crumbs
2 eggs, lightly beaten
3 tablespoons evaporated milk
1/4 cup finely chopped onion
1/4 cup finely chopped green bell pepper
2 cloves garlic, crushed
1 tablespoon Tabasco™
1/2 teaspoon fresh cracked black pepper
1/2 teaspoon salt
vegetable oil for frying
4 sesame buns or hamburger buns
lettuce
tomato
tartar sauce

1. Combine ground conch, bread crumbs, eggs, evaporated milk,

DID YOU KNOW?

Interesting Keys facts:
*The area code for all the Keys is 305.
*There are 42 bridges connecting the Keys. The longest being scenic Seven-mile bridge at 35,716 feet and the shortest is Harris Gap at 37 feet.
*The highest elevation in the Keys is Windley Key at 18 feet above sea level.
*Population from Key West to Key Largo is about 80,000.
*U.S. Highway 1 begins at Fort Kent, Maine, and ends in Key West, Florida (Mile Marker 1)

onion, bell pepper, garlic, Tabasco™, black pepper and salt in a large bowl. Form into four patties.

2. Heat 1/4-inch of vegetable oil in a large, heavy skillet until 350º.

3. Fry conch burgers on each side until golden and vegetables are cooked. Drain on food-grade white paper towels.

4. Arrange burgers on buns, topping with lettuce, tomato and tartar sauce.

BLUE CRAB BURGERS

Region: Miami—Gold Coast
Yield: 4 servings

   1 pound cooked blue crab meat
 3/4 cup plain bread crumbs
 1/2 teaspoon salt
 1/2 teaspoon fresh cracked black pepper
   2 garlic cloves, crushed
   2 large eggs, lightly beaten
 1/4 cup mayonnaise
 1/4 cup chopped fresh parsley
   2 tablespoons finely chopped yellow onion
   2 tablespoons fresh lime or lemon juice
   1 teaspoon Worcestershire™ sauce
 1/4 teaspoon paprika
 1/4 cup flour
vegetable oil for frying

   4 sesame or hamburger buns
   4 slices yellow cheese (any)
lettuce
tomato
tartar sauce

1. Combine crab, bread crumbs, salt, pepper, garlic, eggs, mayonnaise, parsley, onion, lemon juice, Worcestershire™ and paprika in a large bowl. Form into four patties.

2. Heat 1/4 inch of vegetable oil in a large skillet until 350º. Dredge patties in flour, then fry each side until golden. Drain on food-grade white paper towels. Reserve in warm oven.

3. Broil cheese slices on one half of each of the buns until melted. Top each half with a crab burger. Garnish with lettuce, tomato and tartar sauce. Top with remaining buns.

NOTE: Some recipes call for butter in the preceding recipe. I find it burns too easily. If you want the butter flavor though, add a tablespoon to the oil you use to fry the crab burgers.

Paradise Fish and Seafood

FLORIDA HAS some of the best sport fishing in the world. So naturally, you'll find fish and shellfish of every sort in restaurants and home kitchens. The resulting recipes are incredible because the fish is so fresh.

I'm originally from Pembroke, Massachusetts, near Plymouth (home of John Alden, one of the pilgrims on the Mayflower) and Cape Cod. Naturally, access to fish is readily available because of the proximity to the coast.

While I enjoy dinners out with my family: Hans, my father; Tanya, my sister; and my mother, Christa; I must say the fish courses are bland and swimming in butter. It's as if the chefs are afraid to use any seasoning.

I keep an entire pantry stocked with spices and dried herbs. I have herbs growing on my front patio. Yes, I do live in the Caribbean, but it's quite easy to grow herbs on a windowsill year around.

The seafood recipes in this chapter are much improved by the liberal use of Caribbean and Cuban seasonings. Don't be afraid to substitute. If you don't have one herb or spice, use another. If you use shrimp instead of lobster, all the better! After all, that's how most of these recipes came about—improvisation.

THE RECIPES

Lime-Coconut Fried Lobster

Island-Style Curried Lobster with Coconut

Stuffed Grouper Miami-Style

Sour Cream and Mushroom-Stuffed Grouper

Spinach, Mushroom and Seafood Lasagna

Dolphin Baked in Mango Tupelo honey (substitute regular honey)

Cuban Dolphin

Basic Baked Fish Florida-Style

Lime-Baked Dolphin with Garlic and Parsley Potatoes

Easy Seafood and Mushroom Casserole

Scallops, Shrimp and Crab in Smokey Cheese Sauce

Grilled Wahoo with Pineapple and Walnut Salsa with Cinnamon Plantains

Grilled Yellowtail Snapper with Black Bean, Mango and Coconut Salsa

Caribbean Baked Snapper

Snapper in Creole Sauce

Seafood Linguine in Broccoli and Parmesan Lime Butter Sauce

Parmesan Shrimp

Coconut Shrimp

Spicy Egg Batter Shrimp

SHRIMP DIABLO

TANGY CRAB CASSEROLE

SPICY SHRIMP PASTA WITH COCONUT AVOCADO BUTTER

CONCH REPUBLIC SHRIMP BOIL WITH MANGO, KEY LIME MUSTARD SAUCE

GRILLED TUNA WITH CUBAN BLACK BEAN AND MANGO RELISH

GRILLED TUNA WITH HORSERADISH AND GUAVA SAUCE

SPICY FISH TACOS WITH JALAPEÑO CREAM WITH ROASTED GARLIC SALSA

LIME-COCONUT FRIED LOBSTER

Region: Miami, Gold Coast
Yield: 4 servings

Sound too rich to be true? Lightly frying lobster seals in that wonderful sweet flavor and keeps it from drying out. Be sure to heat the oil to 350°, otherwise the batter will soak up too much oil. Also, do not overcrowd pan, as this will lower oil temperature as well.

 4 Florida or Caribbean lobster tails
 juice of 2 Key limes, limes or lemons (4 to 6 tablespoons)
 1/2 cup evaporated milk (unsweetened)
 1/2 cup unsweetened coconut milk
 2 eggs, beaten
 1 cup all-purpose flour
 1 teaspoon salt
 1/2 teaspoon fresh cracked black pepper

 3/4 cup packaged unsweetened shredded coconut
 vegetable oil for frying

1. Remove meat from shell and slice down center back (but not all the way through) with the tip of a sharp knife. Drizzle with lime juice, cover and place in a non-reactive glass-baking dish to marinate for 30 minutes.

2. Combine evaporated milk, coconut milk and eggs in a small bowl. Set aside. Combine flour, salt and black pepper in another bowl. Place shredded coconut in a third bowl.

3. Heat 1/2-inch of oil in a large skillet to 350°.

4. Dip lobster tails in flour, then egg, then shredded coconut. Shake off excess.

5. Fry tails two at time until golden on both sides, about five to eight minutes. Drain on food-grade white paper towels.

6. Serve at once with drawn butter, mustard sauce or chutney.

ISLAND-STYLE CURRIED LOBSTER WITH COCONUT

Region: Florida—Caribbean
Yield: 4 servings

1 1/2 pounds cooked lobster meat
2 tablespoons olive oil
1 small onion, finely chopped
1 small red bell pepper, finely chopped
2 garlic cloves, crushed
2 tablespoons raisins
1 tablespoon grated fresh ginger
1 tablespoon curry powder
1/2 cup unsweetened coconut milk
1/2 cup chicken stock
1/4 cup packaged unsweetened shredded coconut
2 tablespoons dark rum
3 tablespoons butter
2 tablespoons flour
1/4 cup whole milk
1/2 teaspoon paprika

HOT RICE

1. Sauté lobster meat in the olive oil for one minute over moderate heat. Stirring constantly add onion, bell pepper and garlic. Cook until onion is soft, about five minutess.

2. Fold in raisins, ginger and curry powder. Cook for one minute. Pour in coconut milk and chicken stock. Whisk in shredded coconut and rum and lower heat to a bare simmer.

3. Melt butter in a small skillet over medium-high heat. Whisk in flour and cook, stirring constantly for 10

DID YOU KNOW?

Ybor City was once known as the Cigar Capital of the World. Ybor City is one of three National Historic Landmark areas in Florida. Part of Tampa's Latin quarter, this city has charming cobblestone streets and wrought iron balconies.

Cubans brought cigar making to the city in 1886—12,000 tabaqueros (cigar makers) in some 200 factories. Today the smell of hand-rolled cigars by Cuban immigrants delightfully permeates the quarter.

minutes until a roux is formed. Mixture should smell nutty and be golden brown. Stir in milk gradually. Add paprika. Whisk this into lobster mixture and remove from heat.

4. Preheat oven to 375º. Transfer to a 8-inch square glass-baking dish. Bake for 20 minutes, until bubbly. Serve with hot rice.

STUFFED GROUPER MIAMI-STYLE

Region: Miami—Gold Coast
Yield: 4 servings

    2 pounds grouper, dolphin or mahi-mahi
       fillets
    1 tablespoon olive oil
    1 cup finely chopped onion
    4 garlic cloves crushed
  1/4 cup melted butter
    1 cup seasoned stuffing (dry)
    2 tablespoons chopped, pimento-stuffed
       olives

    1 cup diced shrimp
    1 large tomato, thinly sliced
  1/4 cup grated Parmesan
       fresh cracked black pepper

1. Cut a slit in the side of each fish fillet with the tip of a sharp knife. Set aside.

2. Sauté onion and garlic in the olive oil in a medium skillet over moderate heat until soft about five minutes. Add melted butter, stuffing, olives and shrimp. Stir until stuffing is lightly browned. Remove from heat and allow to cool for five minutes.

3. Preheat oven to 350º. If using a convection oven, reduce heat to 325º. Lightly oil the bottom of a 13 x 9 x 2-inch glass-baking dish.

4. Stuff fish fillets, dividing filling evenly between fish fillets. Arrange on baking dish. Top with tomato slices. Sprinkle Parmesan and black pepper over top. Bake for 30 minutes until fish flakes easily.

SOUR CREAM AND MUSHROOM STUFFED GROUPER

Region: Northeast
Yield: 4 servings

  2 pounds grouper, dolphin or mahi-mahi fillets
  1 tablespoon olive oil
  1 cup finely chopped onion
  1 cup sliced mushrooms
  4 garlic cloves, crushed
  1 cup seasoned bread crumb stuffing
  1/2 teaspoon paprika
  1/2 cup sour cream
  1 large tomato, thinly sliced
  1/4 cup grated Parmesan
  fresh cracked black pepper

1. Cut a slit in the side of each fillet with the tip of a sharp knife. Set aside.

2. Sauté onion, garlic and mushrooms in the olive oil in a medium skillet over moderate heat until soft. Add bread crumbs, cooking until lightly browned. Remove from heat and allow to cool for five minutes. Fold in sour cream and paprika. Set aside.

3. Preheat oven to 350°. Lightly oil a 13 x 9 x 2-inch glass-baking dish. Arrange fish fillets on dish and bake for 20 minutes.

4. Remove from oven, cool for five minutes, then stuff with sour cream filling. Arrange tomato slices over fish, sprinkling with Parmesan and black pepper until cheese is golden and bubbly.

5. Return to oven for 10 to 12 minutes.

SPINACH, MUSHROOM AND SEAFOOD LASAGNA

Region: Panhandle
Yield: 6 to 8 servings

Look for the freshest, ripest tomatoes you can find for the topping on this lasagna. I prefer the rich flavor of plum tomatoes. Of course, if you have tomatoes from your garden or the local farmer's market, use those. Ensure good results by purchasing a high-quality jarred marinara sauce.

  1 pound lasagna noodles, boiled and cooled, separated by sheets of waxed paper
  1 tablespoon olive oil
  1/2 cup finely chopped onion
  4 garlic cloves, crushed
  1 cup sliced mushrooms
  2 tablespoons chopped fresh basil
  2 teaspoons dried Italian seasoning
  1/2 cup chopped sun-dried tomatoes packed in oil

1 jar marinara sauce
1 pound dolphin, mahi-mahi or grouper, diced
1/2 pound cooked shrimp, tails removed and diced
1/2 pound scallops
3 cups chopped fresh spinach (substitute 2 packages of frozen, drained)
1 cup shredded mozzarella
6 plum tomatoes cut in 1/4 inch slices
1 cup grated Parmesan cheese
1/2 cup seasoned bread crumbs

1. Sauté onion, garlic and mushrooms in the olive oil in a medium skillet over moderate heat until onions are lightly browned and vegetables softened. Fold in basil, Italian seasoning and sun-dried tomatoes. Set aside.

2. Spread about 1/2 cup of the marinara sauce on the bottom of a lasagna dish (13 x 9 x 2-inch).

3. Preheat oven to 350º.

4. Arrange a layer of noodles to cover bottom of dish.

5. Combine remaining marinara sauce and onion-mushroom mixture. Spread a thin layer of marinara mixture over noodles. Top with one-third of the shrimp, scallops and fish. Top with one-third of spinach, then one-third of mozzarella. Repeat ending with a layer of the marinara mixture.

6. Top with tomato slices. Combine Parmesan and bread crumbs in a small bowl. Sprinkle over tomatoes.

7. Top with foil and bake for 35 minutes. Remove foil and allow cheese to brown for about 10 minutes. Remove from oven and cool for 20 minutes.

MANGO DOLPHIN BAKED IN TUPELO HONEY

Region: The Keys
Yield: 4 servings

- 1/2 cup Tupelo honey (substitute regular honey)
- juice of 1 Key lime, lime or a lemon (2 to 3 tablespoons)
- 1/2 cup white wine
- 1/4 cup orange liqueur, such as Cointreau™, Triple Sec™ or Grand Marnier™
- 1 cup fresh diced mango
- 1/4 teaspoon ground cinnamon
- 2 pounds dolphin fillets
- salt
- pepper

1. Preheat oven to 350°. Combine Tupelo honey, lime juice, wine, orange liqueur, mango and cinnamon in a medium bowl.

2. Lightly oil the bottom of a 13 x 9 x 2-inch glass-baking dish. Arrange dolphin fillets over bottom. Top with mango mixture. Bake for 30 minutes until fish flakes easily.

3. Season to taste with salt and pepper.

CUBAN DOLPHIN

Region: Miami—Cuban
Yield: 4 servings

- 4 dolphin fillets (about 2 pounds)
- juice of 1 Key lime (2 tablespoons)
- 1 large yellow onion, thinly sliced
- 1 green bell pepper, diced
- 4 garlic cloves, crushed
- 2 firm, yet ripe large tomatoes, diced
- 1/4 cup diced pimento-stuffed olives
- 4 tablespoons butter
- 1/4 cup all-purpose flour
- 1 1/2 cups whole milk
- 1/2 cup evaporated milk
- 1 tablespoon Tabasco™
- 3 garlic cloves, crushed
- 1 teaspoon dried Italian seasoning
- 1/2 teaspoon paprika
- 1/2 teaspoon salt
- fresh cracked black pepper

1. Lightly oil a 13 x 9 x 2-inch glass-baking dish. Arrange fish fillets on bottom and drizzle with lime juice.

2. Spread onion slices, bell pepper, garlic and tomatoes over fish. Top with olives. Set aside to marinate, uncovered for no longer than an hour.

3. Melt butter in a medium saucepan over moderate heat. Sprinkle in flour, stirring constantly for 10 minutes to make a roux. Mixture should be light brown.

4. Preheat oven to 350°.

5. Gradually whisk in whole and evaporated milk, stirring constantly until thickened.

6. Fold in Tabasco™, garlic, Italian seasoning, paprika and salt. Pour over fish. Bake for 30 minutes until fish flakes easily.

7. Season to taste with cracked black pepper. Serve with hot, cooked rice and peas.

BASIC BAKED FISH FLORIDA-STYLE

Region: Gulf Coast
Yield: 4 servings

3 pounds grouper, dolphin, mahi-mahi, snapper or other lean fish
juice of 2 Key limes, limes or lemons (4 to 6 tablespoons)
1 tablespoon Worcestershire™ sauce
1 tablespoon olive oil
1/2 teaspoon dried oregano
1/4 teaspoon dried thyme
1 teaspoon sea salt
1/2 teaspoon fresh cracked black pepper
1 small onion, thinly sliced

1. Rinse fish under cool, running water and pat dry. Rub with lime juice and set aside, uncovered, to marinate for 20 minutes.

2. Preheat oven to 375°. Lightly oil the bottom of a 13 x 9 x 2-inch glass-baking dish.

3. Combine Worcestershire™, olive oil, oregano, thyme, sea salt and black pepper in a small bowl.

4. Transfer fish fillets to baking dish. Arrange onion slices over top of fish. Drizzle Worcestershire™ mixture over fish. Bake for 20 to 25 minutes.

DID YOU KNOW?

Gatorade was developed in 1967 for the University of Florida's football team, the Gators. The idea was to create a drink that would fight dehydration and fatigue. That very season, the team, fortified with Gatorade, became known as the 'second half team' because they outplayed their opponents in the final half.

LIME-BAKED DOLPHIN WITH GARLIC AND PARSLEY POTATOES

Region: Miami, Gold Coast
Yield: 6 servings

- 3 pounds dolphin (substitute grouper or mahi-mahi)
- 2 tablespoons olive oil
- 1/2 teaspoon dried thyme
- 1/2 teaspoon dried basil
- 1/2 teaspoon dried Italian seasoning
- juice of 1 lime (reserve fruit for lime rind)
- 6 to 8 new, red potatoes (about 2-inch diameter), skin on
- 1 tablespoon olive oil
- 1 medium onion, finely chopped
- 4 large garlic cloves, crushed
- 2 tablespoons butter
- 3/4 cup chopped fresh parsley
- 1 teaspoon grated fresh lime rind
- 1/4 cup (1/2 stick) butter, melted
- 1/4 teaspoon cayenne pepper
- fresh cracked black pepper
- 1 lime, cut in wedges

1. Rinse fish and pat dry. Lightly oil the bottom of a 13 x 9 x 2-inch glass-baking dish. Arrange fish on bottom.

2. Combine the 2 tablespoons of olive oil with the thyme, basil, Italian seasoning and lime juice. Drizzle over fish and set aside to marinate, uncovered, for 20 minutes.

3. Preheat oven to 350°.

4. Boil potatoes in a medium saucepan for five minutes. Remove from water and cool. Slice potatoes in half.

5. Bake fish for 25 to 30 minutes, until it flakes easily.

6. Heat remaining 1 tablespoon of olive oil in a large, deep skillet. Sauté onion and garlic until soft. Add butter and potato halves, stirring often until potatoes are lightly browned. Remove from heat.

7. Whisk together parsley, lime rind, cayenne and melted butter. Spread evenly over top of fish. Sprinkle with cracked black pepper. Serve with lime wedges.

EASY SEAFOOD AND MUSHROOM CASSEROLE

Region: Northeast, Fernandina Beach
Yield: 6 servings

Use leftover fish and pre-cooked shrimp or lobster for those nights when time is short.

SCALLOPS

The scallop is a bivalve marine mollusk, a.k.a. a shellfish. Scallops grow slowly. The colder the water, the more time it takes for scallops to mature—up to seven years. The great scallop is found in the eastern Atlantic and Mediterranean. The Atlantic deep-sea scallop, the Iceland scallop, and the bay scallop are all part of the queen scallop species. The Atlantic deep-sea scallop is the largest of the scallop family, measuring 6 to 12 inches in diameter. It's also the most commercially important scallop.

Purchasing: Scallops spoil quickly, so you'll find them displayed on a bed of ice. If you don't know if a scallop is thawed or defrosted, ask. Defrosted scallops must be cooked before refrozen. Choose packages of frozen scallops free of frost.

Serving: Scallops can be eaten raw or cooked. I like them pickled as a ceviche in citrus juices. Scallops can be served with rice or pasta, baked, broiled, fried or sautéed.

Storing: Store no longer than one or two days in a closed container in the refrigerator. May be frozen for several months. Cook frozen scallops without defrosting first for peak flavor.

Nutrition info: High in protein, low in fat and carbohydrates.

---

2 pounds pre-cooked grouper, snapper or dolphin fillets, cubed

1 1/2 pounds cooked shrimp, deveined, tails off and diced

1/2 pound scallops

1 1/2 cups frozen peas

2 cans condensed mushroom soup

1 tablespoon Tabasco™

1/4 cup (1/2 stick) melted butter

2 tablespoons light or gold rum

2 cups crumbled Saltine™ crackers

1. Preheat oven to 350º. Lightly oil the bottom of a 13 x 9 x 2-inch glass-baking dish.

2. Arrange fish cubes, shrimp and scallops over bottom of dish. Arrange peas around fish fillets. Combine Tabasco™ and soup. Pour over seafood and peas. Set aside.

3. Heat butter and rum in a medium skillet over moderate heat. Stir in cracker crumbs until golden.

4. Spread cracker mixture over top of fish. Cover with foil and bake for 20 minutes. Remove foil and bake additional 10 minutes until fish flakes easily.

SCALLOPS, SHRIMP AND CRAB IN SMOKEY CHEESE SAUCE

Region: The Keys
Yield: 6 servings

Feel free to substitute any portion of the shrimp, scallops or crab for a less costly fillet of dolphin, snapper or grouper.

- 3 tablespoons butter
- 1/4 cup all-purpose flour
- 1/2 teaspoon paprika
- 1 cup chicken stock
- 1/4 cup dry sherry
- 1/2 cup evaporated milk
- 1 tablespoon Tabasco™
- 2 cups broccoli florets
- 2 pounds assorted, cleaned seafood (scallops, shrimp, crab, firm white fish)
- 1 cup grated, smoked Gouda
- salt
- fresh cracked black pepper

1. Melt butter in a medium saucepan over moderate heat. Whisk in flour and paprika, stirring constantly for 10 minutes until a roux is formed and mixture is light brown.

2. Pour in chicken stock gradually. Keep stirring. Add evaporated milk, sherry, and Tabasco™. Cook for one minute. Remove from heat.

3. Preheat oven to 350º. Lightly grease a 13 x 9 x 2-inch glass-baking dish. Arrange seafood over bottom of dish. Pour chicken stock sauce over fish. Bake for 20 minutes until fish flakes easily.

PLANTAINS

Purchasing: Choose fruit that is firm. Can be green, it will just take time to ripen.

Serving: When unripe, the plantain is similar to a vegetable. When ripe, like a banana, but must be cooked. Use with soups, stews, yams, apples, sautéed and served with fish or roast chicken.

Cooking: Sauté peeled, sliced plantain in a skillet with a little olive oil or butter. May be baked in its skin (wash outside with soap and water first) at 350ºF for about 45 minutes to an hour; or grilled 4 inches above coals for about 3five minutes.

Storing: A green plantain can take two weeks to ripen. Keep at room temperature. When nearly black, and not ready to cook, they will keep another day in the refrigerator. You can also freeze ripe fruits. Peel first, wrap securely in waxed paper.

Nutritional info: Like bananas, high in potassium, Vitamin C, Vitamin B6, magnesium and folic acid.

4. Steam broccoli florets lightly about six minutes. Arrange florets around fish. Sprinkle with grated Gouda. Return to oven for 10 minutes until cheese is bubbly. Season to taste with salt and black pepper. Serve at once.

GRILLED WAHOO WITH PINEAPPLE WALNUT SALSA AND CINNAMON PLANTAINS

Region: Gulf Coast
Yield: 6 servings

If you're a fan of bananas, especially cooked bananas, such as Banana's Foster, you'll love these Cinnamon Plantains.

- 1/2 cup extra-virgin olive oil
- juice of 2 Key limes, limes or lemons (4 to 6 tablespoons)
- 4 tablespoons soy or tamari sauce
- 2 tablespoons grated fresh ginger
- 1 teaspoon toasted sesame oil
- 6 (6-ounce) fillets Wahoo or other firm white fish

SALSA
- 1/2 cup chopped walnuts, lightly toasted
- 1 cup fresh diced pineapple
- 1 large ripe tomato, diced
- 1 small onion, finely chopped
- 1/2 cup chopped fresh cilantro
- 1/4 cup finely chopped green bell pepper
- 2 tablespoons golden raisins
- 1/4 cup extra-virgin olive oil
- 4 tablespoons cider vinegar
- 2 tablespoons balsamic vinegar
- 1 teaspoon dried Italian seasoning
- 1/2 teaspoon salt
- 1/2 teaspoon fresh cracked black pepper

PLANTAINS
- 2 large ripe plantains
- 2 tablespoons butter
- ground cinnamon

1. Combine olive oil, lime juice, soy sauce, ginger and sesame oil in a 13 x 9 x 2-inch glass-baking dish. Marinate fish fillets, uncovered, for one hour.

2. Toast walnut pieces under broiler until fragrant and lightly browned. Do not burn! Remove from oven and set aside.

SALSA
1. Combine pineapple, tomato, onion, cilantro, bell pepper, raisins, olive oil, vinegars, Italian seasoning, salt and black pepper in a medium, non-reactive bowl. Fold in walnut pieces. Cover with plastic wrap and refrigerate.

PLANTAINS
1. Peel plantains and slice in diagonal, 1-inch thick slices. Lightly sprinkle with cinnamon. Melt butter and

sauté plantain over medium heat on both sides until golden. Drain on food grade white paper towels. Reserve in warm oven.

2. Preheat grill for 10 minutes to medium-high heat. Grill fish for five to seven minutes on each side.

3. Serve with chilled Pineapple Walnut Salsa and Cinnamon Plantains.

GRILLED YELLOWTAIL SNAPPER WITH BLACK BEAN, MANGO AND COCONUT SALSA

Region: Florida—Caribbean
Yield: 6 servings

- 1/2 cup finely chopped onion
- 2 large cloves garlic, crushed
- 1/2 cup olive oil
- juice of 2 Key limes (4 tablespoons)
- 1 tablespoon balsamic vinegar
- 1 tablespoon light, gold or dark rum
- 1/2 teaspoon salt
- 1/2 teaspoon fresh cracked black pepper
- 2 pounds yellowtail snapper fillets

SALSA

- 1 cup cooked black beans (firm, not mushy)
- 1 cup fresh diced mango
- 1/2 cup finely chopped onion
- 1 small ripe tomato, diced
- 1/2 cup packaged unsweetened shredded coconut
- 1/4 cup chopped fresh cilantro
- 1/4 cup olive oil
- 1/4 cup cider vinegar
- 1 tablespoon Tupelo honey (substitute regular honey)
- 1/2 teaspoon ground cinnamon
- 1/2 teaspoon salt
- 1/2 teaspoon fresh cracked black pepper

1. Combine onion, garlic, olive oil, lime juice, vinegar, rum, salt and black pepper in a small bowl. Arrange fish fillets on the bottom of a 13 x 9 x 2-inch glass-baking dish. Pour marinade over top and allow to sit for one hour.

SALSA

1. Combine black beans, mango, onion, tomato, coconut, cilantro, olive oil, vinegar, Tupelo honey, cinnamon, salt and black pepper in a large, non-reactive bowl. Cover with plastic wrap and refrigerate.

2. Preheat grill for 10 minutes to medium-high heat. Grill snapper for five minutes on each side, until fish flakes easily.

3. Serve with Black Bean, Mango and Coconut Salsa.

CARIBBEAN BAKED SNAPPER

Region: Florida—Caribbean
Yield: 4 servings

1/2 cup olive oil
1/4 cup dry sherry
1/4 cup white wine
juice of 3 limes or lemons (6 to 8 table spoons)
1 tablespoon cider vinegar
2 tablespoons tomato paste
3 garlic cloves, crushed
1 teaspoon dried Italian seasoning

3 pounds snapper fillets
1 bay leaf
2 large yellow onions, thinly sliced
2 large ripe tomatoes, thinly sliced
2 green bell peppers, diced
1/4 cup pimento-stuffed green olives, chopped
2 tablespoons capers

1. Combine olive oil, sherry, white wine, lime juice, vinegar and tomato paste in a small, non-reactive bowl. Fold in garlic and Italian seasoning. Set aside.

2. Place snapper fillets in a 13 x 9 x 2-inch glass-baking dish. Place bay leaf in dish. Arrange onions, tomatoes, bell pepper, olives and capers over fish. Drizzle with wine sauce.

3. Preheat oven to 375°. Bake 20 to 25 minutes until fish flakes easily.

SNAPPER IN CREOLE SAUCE

Region: Central Florida, Deep South
Yield: 6 servings

You may substitute any firm, white fish for the snapper.

    3 pounds snapper fillets
juice of 2 Key limes (4 tablespoons)
    3 tablespoons butter, softened
salt
pepper
    1 tablespoon olive oil
    1 medium yellow onion, finely chopped
    1 small green bell pepper, diced
    1 large clove garlic, crushed
    1 small stalk celery
  1/2 small hot pepper, habañero or jalapeño,
       seeded and finely chopped
    2 tablespoons butter
    2 tablespoons flour
    1 (14.5-ounce) can stewed tomatoes with
       juice

1. Line a 13 x 9 x 2-inch glass-baking dish with foil. Rinse fish under cool water, pat dry, sprinkle with lime juice, dot with butter and season to taste with salt and pepper.

2. Preheat oven to 400° F. Bake fish for 15 to 20 minutes, until it flakes easily.

3. Meanwhile, sauté onion, bell pepper, garlic, celery and hot pepper in olive oil until vegetables are soft, about five minutes. Add butter, then sprinkle in flour, stirring constantly, cooking for five minutes. Stir in tomatoes, and simmer for 10 minutes. Pour sauce over fish fillets.

SEAFOOD LINGUINE WITH BROCCOLI AND PARMESAN LIME BUTTER SAUCE

Region: Miami—Gulf Coast
Yield: 4 to 6 servings

  1/2 cup walnut pieces
  1/2 teaspoon salt
    4 tablespoon olive oil
  1/2 cup finely chopped onion
    3 garlic cloves, crushed
    3 tablespoons butter
juice of 1 Key lime (2 tablespoons)
    2 teaspoons grated fresh lime rind
  1/2 pound scallops
    1 pound linguine
    2 cups broccoli florets
    1 pound cooked shrimp, deveined, tails off
  1/2 pound diced, cooked lobster or crab,
       picked over for bones
  1/2 cup grated Parmesan cheese
  1/2 cup chopped fresh parsley

1. Toast walnut pieces under broiler until fragrant and golden. Remove from oven and set aside to cool.

2. Fill a deep kettle with water and the 1/2 teaspoon of salt. Bring to boil.

3. Meanwhile, sauté onions and garlic in the olive oil over medium heat in a large saucepan until golden. Add butter, lime juice, lime rind and scallops, cooking for three minutes until opaque. Set aside.

4. Add linguine to boiling water, following instructions on package for cooking.

5. Lightly steam broccoli florets, about seven minutes. Remove from heat and set aside, keeping warm.

6. Add shrimp, lobster, and Parmesan to scallop mixture, cooking over low heat, until cheese is melted and seafood is heated through. Remove from heat and keep in warm place.

7. Drain linguine and fold into seafood. Add broccoli florets and toss to coat linguine evenly. Sprinkle with toasted walnuts and parsley.

PARMESAN SHRIMP

Region: Gulf Coast
Yield: 4 servings

  2 pounds medium raw shrimp
  2 tablespoons olive oil
  1 tablespoon butter
  2 teaspoons Tabasco™
  3 large garlic cloves, crushed
1/4 cup finely chopped green onions
  3 tablespoons chopped fresh parsley
1/2 teaspoon fresh cracked black pepper
1/2 teaspoon sea salt
  2 medium ripe tomatoes, thinly sliced
1/4 cup grated Parmesan cheese (do not use bottled kind)
1/4 cup seasoned bread crumbs

1. Shell and devein shrimp. Rinse under cool water and pat dry with clean dish towels. Set aside.

2. Heat olive oil in a medium skillet. Add butter, Tabasco™, garlic and green onions. Sauté for one minute. Fold in shrimp, stirring and cooking additional five minutes. Shrimp will be barely pink, and not cooked entirely. Stir in parsley, black pepper and sea salt. Remove from heat and set aside.

3. Preheat oven to 400°. Transfer shrimp to a 13 x 9 x 2-inch glass-baking dish, reserving butter sauce from shrimp. Top shrimp with tomato slices.

4. Combine bread crumbs and Parmesan cheese. Spoon over shrimp and tomatoes. Pour reserved butter sauce over top.

5. Bake for 12 to 15 minutes until golden. Serve with hot rice and grilled asparagus or a crisp green salad.

COCONUT SHRIMP

Region: The Keys
Yield: 4 servings

    2   pounds medium or large raw shrimp,
        shelled and deveined
    juice of 1 Key lime, lime or lemon (4 to 6
        tablespoons)
    2   tablespoons cider vinegar
    3/4 cup flour
    3/4 cup packaged unsweetened shredded
        coconut
    3/4 cup unsweetened coconut milk
    1   teaspoon salt
    1/2 teaspoon fresh cracked black pepper
    vegetable oil for frying

1. Pour lime juice and vinegar over shrimp in a non-reactive dish. Allow to marinate, uncovered, for 20 minutes.

2. Arrange flour, shredded coconut, and coconut milk separately in three small bowl.

3. Stir salt and black pepper into flour.

4. Dip each shrimp first into flour (shaking off excess), then into coconut milk, then roll in unsweetened shredded coconut.

5. Heat 1/4 inch of the vegetable oil in a large heavy skillet to 350°. Fry shrimp on all sides until golden. Do not crowd skillet, as you will reduce heat of oil, which will result in soggy, greasy shrimp. Frying at high temperatures reduces amount of oil absorbed. Drain on food-grade white paper towels.

6. Serve with mango chutney or mustard sauce. See chapter on Chutneys, Preserves and Sauces.

SPICY EGG BATTER SHRIMP

Region: Northeast, St. Augustine
Yield: 4 servings

If you prefer a lighter fried shrimp, try this recipe. Omit the hot pepper sauce and cayenne for a milder taste.

- 2 pounds medium raw shrimp, shelled and deveined
- juice of 1 Key lime, lime or lemon (2 to 3 tablespoons)
- 2 tablespoons cider vinegar
- 1 1/4 cups all-purpose flour
- 2 teaspoons dried Italian seasoning
- 1 teaspoon salt
- 1 teaspoon cayenne pepper
- 1/2 teaspoon fresh cracked black pepper
- 4 large eggs, beaten
- 2 tablespoons Tabasco™
- vegetable oil for frying

1. Rinse shrimp under cool running water. Pat dry with clean dish towels. Place in a non-reactive baking dish. Drizzle lime juice and vinegar over shrimp. Marinate, uncovered, for 20 minutes.

2. Combine flour, Italian seasoning, salt, cayenne and black pepper in a small bowl. Set aside. Whisk Tabasco™ into beaten eggs in another small bowl.

3. Heat 1/2 inch of oil in a large, heavy skillet until 350°.

4. Dip shrimp first in flour, then in eggs, then in flour again, shaking off excess.

5. Fry on both sides until golden, but not burnt. Drain on food-grade white paper towels. Serve with chutney, hot chili pepper or mustard sauce.

SHRIMP DIABLO

Region: Miami—Gold Coast
Yield: 4 servings

Try one of the new flavored rums in this recipe. There are many interesting ones to choose from: coconut, mango, pineapple, citrus. Substitute 1/4 cup finely chopped bell pepper for the hotter jalapeño, if desired.

    2   tablespoons olive oil
    1   small onion, finely chopped
    1   small jalapeño pepper, finely chopped
    2   large cloves garlic, crushed
    1/2 teaspoon dried oregano
    1/4 teaspoon dried thyme
    1/4 teaspoon ground coriander
    1/4 teaspoon ground cumin
    2   tablespoons butter
    1   teaspoon salt

    1/2 teaspoon fresh cracked black pepper
    2   pounds medium or large shrimp, shelled and deveined
    1/4 cup rum
    2   tablespoons light or gold rum

1. Sauté garlic, jalapeño and onion in the olive oil in a large skillet over moderate heat until onions are just soft, about 3 minutes.

2. Stir in oregano, thyme, coriander and cumin. Cook for one minute. Add butter, salt and black pepper, stirring constantly.

3. Fold in shrimp, stirring and cooking until shrimp are pink and cooked, about five minutes. Stir in the 1/4 cup of rum, cooking one minute.

4. Remove skillet from heat. Float the 2 tablespoons of rum over the top of shrimp. Carefully light the rum. I use one of those long-handled barbecue grill igniters.

TANGY CRAB CASSEROLE

Region: Lake Okeechobee
Yield: 4 to 6 servings

    1 1/2 cup cooked crab meat
    2   tablespoons cider vinegar
    1 1/2 cup uncooked macaroni

1 tablespoon olive oil
1 medium onion, finely chopped
2 cloves or garlic, crushed
1/2 can condensed cream of
mushroom soup
1 tablespoon Tabasco™
1/2 cup sour cream
3 tablespoons plain yogurt
(not low fat kind)
1/2 teaspoon paprika
3/4 cup grated Cheddar cheese
2 medium ripe tomatoes, sliced
1/2 cup seasoned bread crumbs
1/2 cup grated Parmesan cheese

1. Toss the crab with the cider vinegar and marinate, uncovered while preparing recipe.

2. Cook macaroni according to package directions.

3. While macaroni is cooking heat the olive oil in a medium saucepan. Sauté garlic and onion over medium heat until soft, about three to four minutes.

4. Stir in mushroom soup, Tabasco™, sour cream, yogurt and paprika. Remove from heat.

5. Drain macaroni. and toss with mushroom sauce. Transfer into a 13 x 9 x 2-inch glass-baking dish.

6. Preheat oven to 375º.

7. Spread crab over macaroni. Sprinkle with Cheddar. Top with tomato slices.

8. Combine Parmesan and bread crumbs in a small bowl. Sprinkle over tomato slices. Bake 20 to 25 minutes until lightly browned and bubbly.

SPICY SHRIMP PASTA WITH COCONUT AVOCADO BUTTER

Region: Panhandle
Yield: 4 to 6 servings

3 pounds large shrimp, shelled and
deveined
juice of 1 Key lime, lime or lemon (2 to 3
tablespoons)
3 tablespoons cider vinegar
3 tablespoons frozen orange juice
concentrate, thawed
1 tablespoon toasted sesame oil
1 tablespoon soy sauce
1 tablespoon cayenne pepper
1/2 teaspoon ground cumin
1 teaspoon salt
1 teaspoon fresh cracked black pepper
1 tablespoon olive oil

COCONUT AVOCADO BUTTER

  2 large ripe avocados, peeled and pitted

juice of 1 Key lime, lime or lemon
     (2 to 3 tablespoons)

  1 small yellow onion, finely chopped

  2 cloves garlic, crushed

  2 tablespoons chopped fresh cilantro

1/2 cup unsweetened coconut milk

juice of 1 Key lime, lime or lemon

  1 tablespoon olive oil

  1 pound angel hair pasta or pasta of
     choice

1. Combine lime juice, vinegar, orange juice concentrate, sesame oil, soy sauce, cayenne, cumin, salt, black pepper and olive oil in a 13 x 9 x 2-inch glass-baking dish. Toss and coat shrimp with marinade. Set aside for 30 minutes.

COCONUT AVOCADO BUTTER

1. Sprinkle the 2 tablespoons of the lime juice over avocado to keep it from turning brown. In a large bowl, combine onion, garlic, cilantro and coconut milk.

2. Fold in avocado and beat with a hand held mixer until smooth. Drizzle remaining juice of lime over the top of avocado so it won't brown. Press plastic wrap down over the avocado.

3. Heat remaining 1 tablespoon of olive oil in a large heavy skillet over moderate heat. Transfer shrimp and marinade to skillet. Cook, stirring occasionally until shrimp are pink on all sides. About five minutes. Check for doneness on inside by slicing into a shrimp. Remove from heat, cover and place in a warm spot.

4. Cook pasta according to package directions. Drain and toss with the 1 tablespoon of olive oil.

5. Toss pasta with Coconut Avocado butter. Top with shrimp.

CONCH REPUBLIC SHRIMP BOIL WITH MANGO, KEY LIME, MUSTARD SAUCE

Region: The Keys
Yield: 4 to 6 servings

I use a dark beer or ale for a richer, caramel-like flavor.

MANGO, KEY LIME, MUSTARD SAUCE

  1 cup fresh diced mango

juice of 2 limes (4 tablespoons)

1/2 cup Dijon-style mustard

  3 tablespoons sour cream

3 pounds large shrimp, shelled and deveined

2 bottles of beer (flat beer is fine)

1 tablespoon Old Bay Seasoning™ or any other good fish boil

1 bay leaf

1. Combine mango, lime juice, mustard and sour cream in a blender or food processor. Process until smooth. Set aside.

2. Rinse shrimp under cool, running water. Pour beer into a deep kettle or soup pot. Add Old Bay Seasoning™, bay leaf and bring to a boil.

3. Carefully lower shrimp into beer. When beer returns to a boil, shrimp should be pink and cooked through. Remove at once and drain.

4. Serve at once with Mango Key Lime and Mustard Sauce.

GRILLED TUNA WITH CUBAN BLACK BEAN AND MANGO RELISH

Region: Miami—Cuban
Yield: 4 servings

Cilantro and grapefruit add a bright flavor to this traditional Cuban Black Bean relish. In a hurry? Use canned black beans—just rinse them well.

4 (6 to 8) ounce tuna steaks

1/2 cup olive oil

1/4 cup soy sauce

1/4 cup dry sherry

1 tablespoon Tupelo honey (substitute regular honey)

juice of 1 Key lime, lime or lemon (2 to 3 tablespoons)

2 tablespoons cider vinegar

2 tablespoon grated fresh ginger

1 large garlic clove, crushed

CUBAN BLACK BEAN GRAPEFRUIT RELISH

2 cups cooked black beans

1 large grapefruit (pink is nice and high in lycopene), peeled, sectioned, seeded and diced

juice of 3 lemons (9 tablespoons)

1/4 cup light or dark rum

1 tablespoon balsamic vinegar

1 small red onion, finely chopped

1 tablespoon Tupelo honey (substitute regular honey)

1/2 teaspoon salt

1/2 teaspoon fresh cracked black pepper

1/4 teaspoon ground cinnamon

1/4 teaspoon red pepper flakes

1. Rinse tuna steaks under cool running water and pat dry. Arrange in bottom of non-reactive dish. Combine olive

oil, soy sauce, sherry, Tupelo honey, juice of one lime, cider vinegar, ginger and garlic in a small bowl. Pour over tuna steaks, turning to coat on both sides. Set aside to marinate, uncovered for 30 minutes.

RELISH

1. Toss black beans, grapefruit, remaining lemon juice, rum, balsamic vinegar, onion, honey, salt, black pepper, cinnamon and pepper flakes in a small non-reactive bowl. Set aside to allow mingling of flavors.

2. Preheat a barbecue grill to medium hot. Sear tuna steaks on each side for one minute (watching for oily drips of marinade that may flare up), then move to edges of grill where the heat is not as high. Lower lid and grill until medium rare, about five minutes. Grill longer if desired. Remove from heat with a large metal spatula fully slid under each steak to keep it from breaking.

3. Serve with Cuban Black Bean and Mango Salsa.

GRILLED TUNA WITH HORSERADISH AND GUAVA SAUCE

Region: Gulf Coast
Yield: 4 servings

Don't be intimidated by the mention of guava. Exotic fruit jams and preserves of all kinds can be found on grocer's shelves even in the middle of America. In a pinch, substitute apricot preserves.

HORSERADISH AND GUAVA SAUCE

    4 tablespoons mayonnaise
    2 tablespoons prepared white horseradish
    2 tablespoons guava jelly or paste
    1 tablespoon Dijon-style mustard
    1 teaspoon Tupelo honey (substitute regular honey)

    4 (6 to 8) ounce tuna steaks
    1 tablespoon olive oil
    fresh cracked black pepper
    salt

1. Combine horseradish, mayonnaise, guava jelly, mustard and Tupelo honey in a small bowl. Set aside.

2. Preheat a barbecue grill for 10 minutes. Rinse tuna steaks under cool, running water and pat dry. Lightly season with salt and black pepper. Brush with olive oil.

3. Grill tuna about four to five minutes, according to preferred doneness, on each side.

4. Serve with Horseradish and Guava Sauce.

SPICY FISH TACOS WITH JALAPEÑO CREAM AND ROAST GARLIC SALSA

Region: The Keys
Yield: 4 to 6 servings

    1   cup light cream
  1/4   cup sour cream
    2   tablespoons finely chopped jalapeño peppers (adjust more or less to taste)
  1/2   teaspoon paprika
    1   teaspoon sea salt
    1   teaspoon grated fresh lime rind
    6   garlic cloves, roasted, then finely chopped
    1   medium ripe tomato, diced
  1/2   cup fresh diced mango
    2   tablespoons finely chopped red onion
    2   tablespoons chopped fresh cilantro
  1/4   cup olive oil
    4   tablespoons cider vinegar
   16   small flour tortillas
   12   to 16 ounces cooked tuna (to taste), thinly sliced

1. Puree light cream, sour cream, jalapeños, paprika, sea salt and lime rind in a food processor until smooth. Set aside.

2. Toss roasted garlic, tomato, mango, onion, cilantro, olive oil and vinegar in a small bowl. Set aside.

3. Warm tortillas in microwave. Divide tuna slices evenly between tortillas. Spoon roasted garlic mixture evenly over tuna. Fold in ends of tortilla and roll up.

4. Spoon dollop of jalapeño-sour cream mixture over each tortilla. Serve at once.

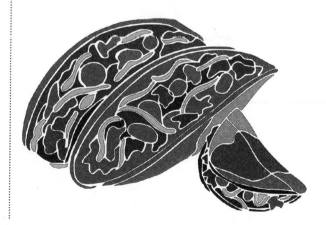

Feelin' Hot, Hot, Hot Chicken and Meat Entrees

IT SEEMS THAT EVERY CARIBBEAN ISLAND and tropical region has its own version of Arroz Con Pollo. Indeed, I can't think of anyone, unless they are vegetarian, who doesn't enjoy this dish.

Both Pilau and Arroz Con Pollo demonstrate Florida's inter-cultural marriage. Two cultures influenced these dishes: Spanish and African. Both combine chicken and or seafood with rice, herbs and spices. The Spanish version is spicier.

Rice plantations prospered in the seventeenth and eighteenth centuries in the lower United States. Settlers from these areas brought mildly seasoned pilau to Florida. Cigar workers in the nineteenth century brought vibrantly spiced arroz con pollo to Florida. Garlic, onion and annatto seed (imparts a smokey flavor and a golden color) make this dish stand out.

In the 1940's and 1950's Arroz Con Pollo was considered an exotic dish to be enjoyed while out on the town. Nowadays you can find it all over Florida, from family get togethers, church picnics to private homes.

THE RECIPES

ARROZ CON POLLO—CUBAN STYLE

ARROZ CON POLLO—PUERTO RICAN STYLE

CHICKEN PILAU

CASHEW-CRUSTED ORANGE CHICKEN

SOUTHERN FRIED CHICKEN

CURRIED CHICKEN

CHICKEN AND HERBED DUMPLINGS

JERKED CHICKEN

SAVORY PAPAYA AND AVOCADO CHICKEN

GARLIC ROAST CHICKEN—CUBAN STYLE

DEEP FRIED WHOLE TURKEY

BARBECUED CHICKEN

CREOLE MARINATED STEAK TIPS

CUBAN-STYLE ROAST PORK

CHORIZO

CUBAN BOLICHE ROAST

BARBECUED BEEF CHUCK

ROPA VIEJA

PICADILLO

TROPICAL MEAT PIE

ARROZ CON POLLO— CUBAN STYLE (YELLOW RICE WITH CHICKEN)

Region: Miami-Cuban
Yield: 8 servings

When I moved to Florida, my Cuban housekeeper turned me on to her version of arroz con pollo. It requires practically no advance planning, and is a perfect way to use up leftover chicken, even turkey.

1 ounce salt pork, finely chopped
   tablespoon olive oil (note if not using saffron, use annatto-infused olive oil (see sidebar)
1 (3 to 4-pound) chicken, cut up with skin on (or assorted breasts and legs)
1 large onion, finely chopped
6 cloves garlic, crushed
1 small red bell pepper, finely chopped
1 small green bell pepper, finely chopped
3 cups long-grain rice
1 (14.5-ounce) can peeled tomatoes, drained and chopped
1/4 teaspoon red pepper flakes
4 cups chicken stock
2 cups beer
1/2 cup dry sherry
12 saffron threads
2 small bay leaves
1 teaspoon fresh cracked black pepper
1/2 teaspoon dried oregano
1/2 teaspoon dried thyme
1 small can peas, drained
1 jar roasted red peppers

1. Heat the salt pork and olive oil in a large deep skillet over moderate heat. Add chicken and brown on all sides. Remove chicken and set aside.

2. Stir in onion, garlic, and bell peppers, sautéing until onion is soft. Fold in rice, cooking for two minutes until rice glistens from the oil. Add tomatoes, pepper flakes, chicken stock, beer and sherry. Bring to a boil, crumble in saffron. Add bay leaves, black pepper, oregano and thyme, stirring for 30 seconds.

ANNATTO-INFUSED OLIVE OIL

It's easy to make your own annatto or achiote-infused olive oil. Use in place of regular olive oil to add an orange hue to food, and complex, smokey flavor.

Heat one part annatto seeds to two parts vegetable oil over moderate heat until oil has turned bright red. Do not overheat oil. Strain and discard seeds.

3. Arrange chicken on top of dish, reduce heat and cover. Simmer until all water is absorbed from rice, about 20 minutes.

4. Turn rice from top to bottom using large forks or spoons. Top with peas and roasted red peppers. Cover and allow to sit for 10 minutes. Serve with fried plantain and a green salad.

ARROZ CON POLLO— PUERTO RICAN STYLE

Region: Florida-Puerto Rican
Yield: 8 servings

There are many good variations of arroz con pollo and you'll find another version of this recipe in *A Taste of Puerto Rico, Too!* published shortly before my move to Miami. Be sure to add the black pepper at the end of cooking, as it will become bitter if cooked too long.

1 (3 to 4-pound) chicken, cut in serving pieces
1 1/2 teaspoons salt
4 tablespoons annatto-infused olive oil (see sidebar page 107)
1 ounce salt pork, finely chopped
2 ounces cooked ham, finely chopped
1 large onion, finely chopped
3 garlic cloves, crushed
2 medium aji dulces (small sweet pepper, substitute any mild pepper), finely chopped
1 red bell pepper
2 ripe tomatoes, chopped
1/2 cup pimento-stuffed olives, chopped
2 tablespoons capers
2 chopped fresh culantro leaves, or 2 tablespoons chopped fresh cilantro, or 2 teaspoons dried
1 teaspoon dried oregano
1 cup tomato sauce
1/4 cup tomato paste
2 cups water
1 cup chicken stock
1/2 cup dry sherry
2 cups long-grain rice
1 large can asparagus spears, drained
1 small can peas, drained
1/4 cup canned pimentos, chopped
salt
fresh cracked black pepper

1. Rinse chicken under cool, running water and pat dry. Season with salt. Set aside.

2. Heat annatto-infused olive oil in a large, covered skillet or Dutch oven over medium heat. Stir in salt pork, and brown lightly for 2 minutes. Add chicken and ham, browning on all sides. Remove chicken, salt pork and ham with a slotted spoon and reserve.

3. Add onion, garlic, aji dulces and bell pepper to skillet. Sauté over medium heat until onion softens, about five minutes. Fold in tomatoes, capers, olives, and culantro, stirring and cooking one minute.

4. Stir in oregano, tomato sauce, tomato paste, chicken stock, water, sherry and reserved chicken. Bring to a boil.

5. Add rice and mix well. When mixture comes to boil again, reduce heat, simmer for 20 minutes until all water is absorbed by rice.

6. Top with asparagus, peas and pimentos. Cover and allow to sit for 15 minutes. Season to taste with salt and black pepper.

MINORCAN SETTLER'S AND DATIL PEPPERS

The Minorcans are to St. Augustine as the Cajuns are to Louisiana. Originally from Greece, Italy and the island of Minorca, the ethnic group came to New Smyrna in 1768 to work on Dr. Andrew Turnbull's indigo plantation.

The Minorcan's tired of Dr. Turnbull's oppressive work conditions and moved to St. Augustine in 1777, after a court hearing freed them from their work obligations. They settled outside of St. Augustine on land offered to them at no charge. Later in 1783, the British returned Florida back to Spain, the Minorcans moved into housing abandoned by the Brits.

Like the Cajuns, Minorcans enjoy spicy food, as evidenced by the regular use of the fiery Datil pepper, which is a prominent ingredient in Minorcan sausage, pilau (rice dishes made with sausage, seafood, meat or chicken) and Minorcan clam chowder.

The Datil pepper is grown almost exclusively in St. Augustine. The Datil pepper is orange-yellow in color and has a pungent unique flavor. It's scoville rating is 300,000—that of the habañera or scotch bonnet is only 100,000—so I can't even begin to imagine how hot this pepper is. For product sources for this pepper, see the Resource section.

CHICKEN PILAU

Region: Northeast—St. Augustine
Yield: 6 servings

Both Arroz con Pollo and Pilau are tasty and simple dishes for the time-harried cook. And who isn't in these days of two-career families? This dish keeps well and actually tastes better the second day. Save even more time by making enough for two meals.

       2   tablespoons olive oil
       1   large onion, finely chopped
       1   (3 to 4-pound) chicken, cut up in
           serving pieces
       2   cups chicken stock
       1   ounce salt pork, finely chopped
       1   large red bell pepper, finely chopped
       3   cloves garlic, crushed
       2   cups long-grain rice
    1/2   cup beer or dry sherry
       1   (14.5-ounce) can stewed tomatoes,
           drained and chopped
       1   teaspoon dried oregano
    1/2   teaspoon dried thyme
       1   teaspoon Datil pepper hot sauce
           (see resources)
           salt and pepper to taste
       1   hard-cooked egg, chopped
    1/4   cup chopped fresh parsley

1. Heat olive oil in a large deep skillet or Dutch oven. Add onion and cook until just barely soft. Brown chicken over medium heat. Add 1 cup of chicken stock, cover and simmer over low heat for 25 to 35 minutes.

2. Remove chicken from pan and set aside. Reserve stock from chicken. Skin chicken and pull meat from bone, discarding bones and skin. Chop meat into bite-sized pieces and set aside.

3. In the same skillet, sauté the salt pork, bell pepper and garlic until pork is browned. Add rice, stir and cook for two minutes, coating rice evenly with the fat.

4. Return reserved chicken stock, remaining one cup of chicken stock and sherry to skillet. Stir in tomatoes, oregano and thyme. Cover and simmer over low heat for 20 minutes.

5. Fold in reserved chicken and the Datil pepper sauce, cover and cook for additional five minutes until rice is heated through. All liquid will have been absorbed by now.

6. Season to taste with salt and pepper. Garnish with chopped egg and parsley.

NOTE: Remember the Datil pepper is fiery hot, hot, hot.

A Taste of Florida

CASHEW-CRUSTED ORANGE CHICKEN

Region: Panhandle
Yield: 4 to 6 servings

   juice of 1 orange (4 tablespoons)
  2 tablespoons fresh grated orange rind
1/2 cup (1 stick) butter, melted
  1 egg, lightly beaten
  1 tablespoon Tupelo honey (substitute regular honey)
3/4 cup crushed Saltine™-style crackers, crushed
1/4 cup finely crushed cashews
  1 teaspoon dried Italian herbs
1/2 teaspoon salt
1/2 teaspoon fresh cracked black pepper
  2 pounds chicken parts, breasts or legs

1. Combine orange juice, peel, butter, egg and Tupelo honey in a shallow dish. Set aside.

2. Combine crushed crackers, cashews, herbs, salt and black pepper in a separate shallow dish.

3. Preheat oven to 400° F.

4. Rinse chicken under cool water and pat dry. Dip chicken in butter-Tupelo honey (substitute regular honey) mixture, then roll in cracker-cashew mixture.

5. Arrange chicken on baking dish. Bake for 35 to 40 minutes until golden and crunchy.

SOUTHERN FRIED CHICKEN

Region: Central Florida, Deep South
Yield: 4 servings

The first food that comes to mind when you think of Southern cooking is fried chicken. If you wish to reduce the fat in this recipe, remove the skin from the chicken.

  1 (3 to 4-pound) frying chicken, cut in serving pieces
  3 to 4 teaspoons Lawry's Seasoned Salt™
1/2 teaspoon dried oregano
  3 garlic cloves, crushed
  1 cup all-purpose flour
vegetable oil for frying

1. Rinse chicken under cool running water, pat dry.

2. Combine Lawry's Seasoned Salt™, oregano and garlic along with flour in a shallow pan or dish.

3. Roll in chicken in seasoned flour, shaking off excess.

4. Heat 1-inch of oil in a frying to 350° F. Fry chicken, taking care not to crowd pan, which would reduce heat of oil and cause chicken to absorb too much fat. Fry until golden and crispy.

5. Drain on food-grade white paper towels.

CURRIED CHICKEN

Region: Florida-Caribbean
Yield: 6 servings

    1   (3 to 4-pound) serving chicken,
        cut in pieces
    1   tablespoon curry powder
  1/2   teaspoon ground cumin
  1/2   teaspoon ground cinnamon
  1/2   teaspoon ground red pepper
    1   tablespoon chicken seasoning
    2   tablespoons olive oil
    1   large onion, finely chopped
    2   large ripe tomatoes, chopped
  3/4   cup chicken stock
  1/4   cup dry sherry
  1/4   cup unsweetened coconut milk
    3   tablespoons flour
    2   tablespoons butter
  1/2   teaspoon hot pepper sauce
        salt
        pepper

1. Rinse chicken under cool, running water, pat dry and set aside.

2. Heat curry powder, cumin, cinnamon, red pepper and chicken seasoning in a large skillet or Dutch oven over moderate heat for one minute until slightly darkened and a fragrant aroma is released.

3. Add olive oil and sauté onion until just soft, about five minutes. Add chicken pieces, tomatoes, stock, sherry and coconut milk. Cover and simmer over moderate heat for 20 minutes.

4. Heat butter in a separate small pot or skillet over moderate heat until melted. Sprinkle in flour, stirring constantly for 10 minutes, until a golden color and a nutty aroma is emitted.

5. Fold this roux into chicken mixture, stirring until thickened. Simmer for seven to eight minutes. Stir in hot pepper sauce. Season to taste with salt and pepper. Serve with fluffy white rice and green vegetables.

CHICKEN AND HERBED DUMPLINGS

Region: Southern Florida—Everglades
Yield: 6 servings

Just like the Caribbean islands, in old days, every Southerner had a chicken coop or at least free-roaming chickens. In Puerto Rico, the chicken coop was like an alarm system, notifying householders of would-be intruders. Some of the birds were wily, and eluded capture until they became old and tough. Stewing these old birds was the best way to make their stringy meat palatable. The rosemary in the dumplings is heavenly, and an excellent antioxidant.

- 1 (3 to 4-pound) chicken, cut in serving pieces
- 1 lemon, quartered
- 1 cup all-purpose flour
- 1 teaspoon salt
- 1 teaspoon ground black pepper
- 1 teaspoon poultry seasoning
- 1/2 teaspoon ground cumin
- 1/4 teaspoon ground cardamom
- 1 tablespoon butter
- 1 tablespoon olive oil
- 1 bay leaf
- 1 large onion, coarsely chopped
- 3 large carrots, cut in 2-inch pieces
- 2 parsnips, cut in 2-inch pieces
- 2 large stalks celery, diced
- 3 cups chicken stock
- 1/2 cup dry sherry
- 1/2 cup apple cider or juice

DUMPLINGS

- 1 1/2 cups all-purpose flour
- 1/2 cup cornmeal
- 1 tablespoon baking powder
- 1/2 teaspoon salt
- 1 teaspoon chopped fresh rosemary
- 1/4 teaspoon ground nutmeg
- 1 cup half-and-half
- 3 tablespoons butter, melted

1. Rinse chicken under cool running water and pat dry. Squeeze lemons over chicken and set aside.

DID YOU KNOW?

Naples is considered the Palm Beach of the Gulf Coast. 21 miles south of Bonita Springs. Thirty years ago Naples was the epitome of Old Florida with its pastel stucco buildings, bungalows and stunning beaches. Nowadays, Naples glitters with multi-story condominiums, upscale eateries, and oh-so-sophisticated shopping Meccas such as tree-lined Fifth Avenue South, Waterside Shops and the Village on Venetian Bay.

2. Combine flour, salt, black pepper, poultry seasoning, cumin, and cardamom in a shallow dish. Dredge chicken in seasoned flour, shaking off excess. Set aside.

3. Heat butter and olive oil in a large covered skillet or Dutch oven over medium-high heat. Add bay leaf, onion, carrots, parsnips and celery. Stirring constantly, add chicken stock, sherry and apple cider and bring to a boil. Reduce heat to simmer, cover and cook for 15 minutes until chicken is cooked. Remove from heat to cool.

4. When chicken is cool, remove skin and discard. Remove meat from bone, dice into bite-sized pieces and return to vegetables.

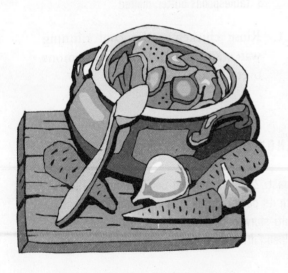

DUMPLINGS

1. Stir sift together flour, cornmeal, baking powder and salt in a medium bowl. Fold in rosemary and nutmeg.

2. Whisk in half-and-half and melted butter to form a stiff dough.

3. Scoop up dumplings using a large spoon and drop into chicken mixture. Simmer in chicken stock, covered for 10 to 12 minutes until dumplings are done. Discard bay leaf.

JERKED CHICKEN

Region: Florida-Caribbean
Yield: 6 servings

This method of cooking made its way to Florida via Jamaica from the Carib-Arawak Indians. The Indians would line a deep pit with wood and stones, which imparted a smoky flavor to the meat. The small animal or bird was 'jerked' by poking with small holes that would then be stuffed with spices and roasted slowly over low heat. The end result was a wonderfully spicy, moist meat.

1 cup olive oil
1 large onion, finely chopped
2 habañero or Scotch bonnet peppers,
 seeded and finely chopped
2 tablespoons grated fresh ginger
2 teaspoons dried thyme
4 large garlic cloves, crushed
1/2 cup orange juice
1/4 cup cider vinegar
juice of 1 Key lime or regular lime
 (2 tablespoons)
1/4 cup packed brown sugar
1 tablespoon ground allspice
1 teaspoon dried sage
1/2 teaspoon ground cinnamon
1/2 teaspoon ground nutmeg
3 pounds chicken breasts or thighs

1. Combine all ingredients except chicken thighs in a food processor. Place chicken in a glass-baking dish and pour marinade over top, turning chicken to coat evenly. Marinate covered overnight in the refrigerator.

2. Preheat barbecue grill to low to medium heat. Alternatively, set oven to 300º. Barbecue or bake chicken slowly until juices run clear when cut.

SAVORY PAPAYA AND AVOCADO CHICKEN

Region: Florida Caribbean
Yield: 4 servings

1 medium ripe papaya
1 tablespoon olive oil
1 tablespoon Worcestershire™ sauce
2 teaspoons dried Italian seasoning
1 teaspoon sea salt
1/2 teaspoon fresh cracked black pepper
1 tablespoon olive oil
4 boneless skinless chicken breasts,
 coarsely chopped
1 small onion, finely chopped
1 small stalk celery, diced
2 cloves garlic, crushed
1 large ripe avocado

1. Cut papaya in half and scoop out the flesh, discarding the shell and seeds. Puree in a food processor along with the olive oil, Worcestershire™, Italian seasoning, sea salt and black pepper. Set aside.

2. Brown the chicken, onion, celery and garlic in the remaining tablespoon of olive oil in a large skillet over moderate heat, cooking until done, about 12 to 15 minutes. Remove from heat, cover and keep in a warm place.

3. Slice avocado in half, discarding pit. Cut avocado in thin slices and fan out around the edges of a serving plate.

4. Arrange chicken in center of serving plate, surrounded by avocado. Top with papaya sauce.

GARLIC ROAST CHICKEN CUBAN-STYLE

Region: Miami—Cuban
Yield: 6 servings

  1 (3 to 4-pound) chicken
 10 cloves garlic, peeled only
  2 large lemons
paprika
  1 teaspoon salt
  1 teaspoon fresh cracked black pepper
  2 tablespoons olive oil
  2 teaspoons dried oregano
 1/2 teaspoon ground cumin
 1/2 cup fresh lime juice
 1/4 cup frozen orange juice concentrate, thawed
  1 tablespoon chopped fresh oregano, or 1 teaspoon dried

1. Rinse chicken inside and out. Pat dry. Quarter one lemon and place inside body cavity along with 4 cloves of garlic. Cut other lemon in half and rub on outside of chicken.

2. Sprinkle chicken lightly with paprika, then salt, then black pepper. Set aside.

3. Combine olive oil, oregano, cumin, lime juice, frozen orange juice concentrate and oregano in a small bowl. Crush remaining 6 cloves of garlic and add to bowl.

4. Baste chicken with marinade. Cover with plastic wrap and marinate, or at least eight hours, in the refrigerator.

5. Preheat oven to 375º F. Place chicken on a roasting pan, reserving marinade. Bake for 65 to 75 minutes, basting several times with marinade. Remove when done, i.e. juice run clear when the thickest portion of the thigh is pierced.

BARBECUED CHICKEN

Region: Central Florida
Yield: 4 servings

Besides utilizing Caribbean rum, Southerners add flavor to sauces with Kentucky bourbon. The addition of allspice adds a hint of the Caribbean to this recipe.

DID YOU KNOW?

There are more than 17,000 golf courses in the U.S., and **Florida has more than 1,200 golf courses** so you'll never be far from one—with the exception of the Everglades. The most concentrated golf locales are Naples and Palm Beach. In addition, many of these courses will allow you to play without being a member. Just be sure to reserve a tee time in advance.

1/3 cup Kentucky bourbon
1/2 cup soy sauce
3 tablespoons vegetable oil
1 large onion, chopped
4 garlic cloves, crushed
1/2 small jalapeño pepper, chopped
1/2 teaspoon ground allspice
1/2 teaspoon paprika
1/4 teaspoon red pepper flakes
3 to 4 pounds boneless skinless chicken breasts, rinsed under cool, running water

1. Puree bourbon, soy sauce, oil, onion, garlic, jalapeño pepper, allspice, paprika and red pepper flakes in blender. Drizzle over chicken and refrigerate covered for several hours.

2. Preheat barbecue grill and grill chicken for 10 to 15 minutes on each side, basting constantly, or set oven to 350º F, place chicken in a 13 x 9 x 2-inch glass-baking dish and bake for 40 minutes.

CREOLE MARINATED STEAK TIPS

Region: Central Florida, Deep South
Yield: 4 servings

Delicious bourbon sauce accented with savory Creole seasoning. Serve with rice and steamed vegetables.

2 cups Kentucky bourbon
2 pounds lean boneless strip or rib-eye steaks or sirloin
1 small onion, finely chopped
4 garlic cloves, crushed
1 teaspoon paprika
1 teaspoon dried thyme
1/2 teaspoon fresh cracked black pepper
1/2 teaspoon salt
1/4 teaspoon red pepper flakes

1. Cover and marinate steak overnight, or at least eight hours, in bourbon. Remove from marinade and pat dry with paper towels.

2. Combine garlic, onion, paprika, thyme, black pepper, salt and red pepper flakes in a small bowl. Rub into steak.

3. Preheat a barbecue grill, and cook steak evenly on both sides to desired doneness.

4. Slice steak diagonally, in thin strips and serve.

CUBAN-STYLE ROAST PORK

Region: Miami—Cuban
Yield: 12 servings

5 to 6	pound pork roast
12	garlic cloves, thinly sliced
1 1/2	cups orange juice
1	cup fresh lemon juice
1	cup red wine
1/2	cup chopped fresh cilantro, or 3 table spoons dried
2	crumbled bay leaves
1	teaspoon dried oregano
1	teaspoon dried rosemary (whole)

1. Make slits all over the roast with the tip of a sharp knife. Insert garlic.

2. Combine orange juice, lemon juice, wine, cilantro, bay leaves, oregano and rosemary in a small bowl. Pour over roast, cover and marinate overnight, or eight hours, in the refrigerator.

3. Preheat oven to 325° F. Place roast in a Dutch oven and cover. Roast for 3 hours or until a meat thermometer inserted in center of roast reads 165° F.

4. Allow roast to rest for 15 minutes before serving.

CHORIZO

Region: Miami—Cuban
Yield: 4 to 6 servings

Shape the ingredients into patties, or crumble into other dishes.

1 1/2	pounds ground pork or beef
2	tablespoon chili powder
1	teaspoon salt
1/2	teaspoon ground cumin
1/4	teaspoon ground coriander
4	garlic cloves, crushed
3	tablespoons vinegar

1. Fold chili powder, salt, cumin, coriander, garlic and vinegar into ground meat. Place in a glass jar, cover and marinate for 24 hours in refrigerator.

2. Sauté in a large skillet over medium heat until browned. Alternatively, form into patties, then sauté until cooked.

CUBAN BOLICHE ROAST

Region: Florida-Cuban
Yield: 8 to 12 servings

This recipe is half English, half Cuban.

  5   pound eye roast
  1   cup chopped chorizo sausage
  6   garlic cloves, thinly sliced
1/2   cup flour
  1   teaspoon salt
1/2   teaspoon fresh cracked black pepper
  3   tablespoons olive oil
  1   tablespoon olive oil
  1   medium onion, finely chopped
  1   green bell pepper, finely chopped
  2   teaspoons paprika
  1   teaspoon dried oregano
  1   teaspoon dried thyme
  2   crumbled bay leaves
  1   cup tomato sauce

1. Slice roast down the center, about 1-inch deep to make a pocket. Stuff with chorizo. Make slits in roast and insert garlic slices.

2. Combine salt, black pepper and flour, generously dusting roast.

3. Sauté roast in the 3 tablespoons olive oil in a Dutch oven over moderate heat until browned on all sides, about five to seven minutes.

4. Sauté onion and bell pepper in remaining tablespoon olive oil for three to four minutes until soft. Stir in paprika, oregano, thyme, bay leaves and tomato sauce.

5. Baste roast with tomato mixture, cover with lid to Dutch oven and cook over low heat for three hours.

BARBECUED BEEF CHUCK

Region: Northeast Florida
Yield: 6 servings

Barbequing is as popular in the Southern states as it is in the Caribbean. Agreeable weather made outdoor cooking a pleasure and avoids unnecessarily heating up the kitchen. Serve leftovers as hearty sandwich filling. If you prefer not to grill, set oven at 300ºF and roast for one and half hours.

- 1 (3-pound) chuck roast or round
- 1 medium onion, finely chopped
- 4 garlic cloves, crushed
- 3 teaspoons chili powder
- 1 teaspoon salt
- 1/2 teaspoon fresh cracked black pepper
- 3/4 teaspoon dried oregano
- 1/2 teaspoon dried thyme
- 1/4 teaspoon ground cumin
- 2 tablespoons tomato paste
- 1/4 cup fresh lime or lemon juice
- 1/4 cup olive oil
- 1/4 cup light or dark rum

1. Place roast in large plastic bag. Bags expressly for marinating can be purchased at the grocery store.

2. Combine onion, garlic, chili powder, salt, black pepper, oregano, thyme, cumin, tomato paste, olive oil, lemon juice and rum in a small non-reactive bowl.

3. Pour over meat, seal bag and refrigerate overnight.

4. Preheat grill. Remove meat from bag, drain and reserve marinade.

5. Brush meat with marinade, reduce grill to lowest setting, and place meat on grill. Cover grill and cook until meat is tender, about two hours. Be sure to baste with marinade and turn roast occasionally.

6. Do not over cook. Roast is done when a meat thermometer reads between 120 and 150° F, depending upon your preference of doneness.

ROPA VIEJA

Region: Cuban, Puerto Rican
Yield: 6 servings

This meat stew is tasty and quick to prepare. Moreover, it makes the house smell wonderful! Serve with hot white rice, black beans and fried plantains.

- 3 pounds flank steak, cut into 3 by 4 inch strips, or boneless beef round roast
- 3 tablespoons olive oil
- 4 garlic cloves, crushed

SOFRITO

Yield: about 1 1/2 cups

Sofrito is the base of Puerto Rican cooking. You can buy it pre-made, or even better, make your own for a exuberant taste to add to meals. Culantro is similar to cilantro, just about 10 times stronger. Use extra cilantro, or grow your own cilantro on the windowsill. Add sofrito to beans, rice, stews, etc.

1 tablespoon rock or sea salt	1 green bell pepper, diced
1 tablespoon black peppercorns	1 red bell pepper, diced
8 garlic cloves, crushed	1/2 teaspoon dried thyme
1/2 cup chopped fresh cilantro or culantro	1/2 teaspoon dried oregano
6 aji dulces (substitute any mild chile pepper)	1/2 cup olive oil

Using a mortar and pestle and an up and down motion, crush the salt and peppercorns. Add crushed garlic, continuing with up and down motion. You will be making a paste. Mix in culantro or cilantro. Place peppers, thyme, oregano and olive oil in a food processor along with garlic paste. Process until chunky. Place in a Ziploc™ freezer bag; freeze in portions.

1 small onion, finely chopped
1 small green bell pepper, finely chopped
1 cup tomato sauce
1/4 cup vinegar
1 cup water
1 cup sofrito sauce (see following recipe)

1. Heat oil in large skillet and brown meat on all sides. Remove meat from skillet and reserve.

2. Sauté garlic, onion and bell pepper until soft, about five minutes. Stir in tomato sauce, water and sofrito.

3. Return meat to pot, cover and simmer on very, very low heat (about two hours) until meat shreds easily, like old clothes. Add additional water as needed.

PICADILLO

Region: Miami—Cuban
Yield: 2 pounds Picadillo

Picadillo can be used to stuff green bell peppers, served as a dip with corn chips, or rolled in a tortilla.

1 1/2 pounds extra-lean ground beef
1 tablespoon olive oil
4 garlic cloves, crushed

1 large yellow onion, finely chopped
1 green bell pepper, finely chopped
1 jalapeño or other hot pepper, seeded and finely chopped
2 cups canned, crushed tomatoes
1 cup fresh diced or canned pineapple
1/2 cup raisins
12 pimento-stuffed olives, chopped
3 tablespoons vinegar
1 teaspoon packed brown sugar
1/2 teaspoon ground cinnamon
1/2 teaspoon ground cumin
1/2 teaspoon dried oregano

1. Brown beef, olive oil, garlic, onion, bell pepper and hot pepper in a large skillet over medium heat until meat is no longer pink. Drain off excess fat.

2. Add tomatoes, pineapple, raisins, olives, vinegar, sugar, cinnamon, cumin and oregano. Simmer over low heat for 15 minutes.

TROPICAL MEAT PIE

Region: Florida-Caribbean
Yield: 6 to 8 servings

1 tablespoon olive oil
1 small onion, finely chopped
3 cloves garlic, crushed
1 medium green bell pepper, finely chopped
1 pound extra lean ground beef
3/4 cup tomato sauce
2 tablespoons cider vinegar
2 tablespoons finely chopped jalapeño peppers
1 teaspoon salt
1 teaspoon dried oregano
1/2 teaspoon dried thyme
1/2 teaspoon fresh cracked black pepper
3/4 cup grated Cheddar cheese
1 ready-made pie shell

1. Heat olive oil in large skillet over medium heat. Sauté onion, garlic and bell pepper until soft. Crumble in ground beef. Stir constantly until no pink remains. Transfer to a metal or wire colander and rinse off excess fat with hot water. Rinse out skillet with hot water.

2. Return ground beef-onion mixture to skillet. Stir in tomato sauce, vinegar, jalapeño peppers, salt, oregano, thyme and black pepper.

3. Preheat oven to 350°. Transfer ground beef mixture to pie shell. Top with grated cheese.

4. Bake 35 to 45 minutes until crust is golden and cheese is bubbly.

DID YOU KNOW?

Coppertone™ Suntan Cream was based on an invention for soldiers stationed in the South Pacific during World War II by Airman Benjamin Green. Using his wife's stove, he combined cocoa butter and jasmine, and tested the concoction on his head, which really needed it, because Airman Green was bald!

Chutney's, Preserves, and Sauces

CHUTNEYS AND PRESERVES ARE A GOOD way to cut down on kitchen time without sacrificing flavor. Tropical fruits and vegetables lend themselves to zippy condiments. Keep an assortment of chutneys and sauces on hand to dress up fish, poultry, meatloaf, sandwiches and vegetables. Serve tangy chutneys with piquant cheeses and crisp crackers. Be sure to save empty jam and jelly jars, sterilize, then wrap in brightly colored tissue paper for a much appreciated hostess gift.

THE RECIPES

MANGO CHUTNEY

Region: Florida—Caribbean
Yield: about 4 1/2 cups

A wonderful aroma will fill your home when you make this piquant preserve.

- 1 cup cider vinegar
- 1/2 cup packed brown sugar
- 1 large onion, finely chopped
- 1 tablespoon grated fresh ginger
- 1/2 small jalapeño pepper, seeded and finely chopped
- 1 teaspoon curry powder, dry roasted in a small skillet for 3 minutes
- 1/2 teaspoon cayenne pepper
- 4 cups fresh diced mango (about 5 to 6 mangos)

1. Bring vinegar and brown sugar to a boil, lower heat and simmer for 10 minutes.

2. Puree onion, ginger, jalapeño pepper, curry powder and cayenne in a food processor and add to vinegar. Simmer for 10 minutes.

3. Add mango and cook, uncovered over low heat, for 25 minutes. Stir occasionally. Pour into sterilized canning jars, following manufacturers instructions for sealing. Keeps for several months unopened. After opening, refrigerate.

CURRIED PINEAPPLE GLAZE

Region: Central Florida
Yield: about 3 1/2 cups

Spoon over fish, chicken, meat or pork. Try using kudzu instead of cornstarch. It's much easier to work with, and not as lumpy. Find in your local health food store.

- 1 tablespoon olive oil
- 1 small onion, finely chopped
- 2 cups fresh diced pineapple
- 1/2 cup pineapple juice
- juice of 2 Key limes, limes or lemons (4 to 6 tablespoons)
- 1/4 cup sugar
- 1 tablespoon cornstarch or kudzu root
- 1 teaspoon curry powder
- 1/4 cup dark rum

1. Sauté the onion in the olive oil in a medium skillet over medium heat until just soft. Toss in pineapple, stir, cooking for one minute.

2. Add pineapple juice and lime juice, reduce heat, stirring constantly.

3. Combine sugar, cornstarch and curry powder in a cup or small bowl.

4. When mixture attains a boil, gradually sprinkle in sugar mixture. Return heat to medium, stirring constantly until mixture thickens. Remove from heat.

5. Whisk in rum and allow to cool.

LEMON-PAPAYA MARMALADE

Region: Central Florida, Citrus Country
Yield: about 1 1/2 quarts

Choose firm, yellow papayas, with a few green streaks on outside. You want the fruit ripe, but not too soft for the marmalade—it will soften further with cooking.

1/2 cup grated fresh lemon rind
2 cups granulated sugar
2 cups fresh lemon juice
1/2 teaspoon ground cardamom
4 cups slightly under-ripe pulp

1. Heat the lemon rind, sugar and lemon juice to boiling in a large saucepan over medium heat. Simmer for 15 minutes.

2. Fold in cardamom and papaya, stirring constantly, cooking until mixture thickens about 20 minutes.

3. Pour into sterilized canning jars, following manufacturer's instructions.

PAPAYA

Papayas are native to Central America. This fragrant, beta-cartone-rich fruit grows on trees, which attain between 6 and 33 feet, although technically not a tree because its trunk is not woody enough, and leaves only grow on top. (I wondered about that myself). Papaya trees produce up to 150 fruits per annum, producing continuously year-round. Papayas grow all over the sub-tropics and tropics.
Purchasing: I like to choose fruits that are 95% yellow, with a few green streaks. Papayas ripen nicely just out on their own. I wait until all the green is gone, and the outside skin is soft.
Serving: Slice in half and scoop out seeds. You can use these seeds (pureed in a blender) in salad dressing as they are similar in taste to pepper. Drizzle the fruit with fresh lime or lemon juice. Nice with yogurt, oatmeal, or on top of granola.
Nutritional info: Good source of Vitamin C and A. Contains potassium as well. Eighty-nine percent water.

CANDIED GRAPEFRUIT PEELS

Region: Central Florida, Citrus Country
Yield: about 1 pound

Wonderful edible garnish for savory fish, meat or chicken dishes. I use organic grapefruit.

peel from 4 grapefruits
water
  2 cups granulated sugar
  2 tablespoons grated fresh ginger
granulated sugar for rolling

1. Cut peel into 1/4 to 1/2 inch wide strips. Place in a deep saucepan and cover with cold water. Bring to boil, drain and repeat four more times. This will remove any bitterness.

2. Return peel to saucepan; add sugar and just enough water to cover peels. Add ginger and simmer over low heat, stirring often until sugar reaches the soft ball stage 235° F.

3. Remove grapefruit peel, then roll in granulated sugar. Cool, then store in refrigerator in between sheets of waxed paper.

CINNAMON-KUMQUAT MARMALADE

Region: Central Florida, Citrus Country
Yield: about 2 pounds

The kumquat grows on a 16 to 20 foot tree. The fruit is tiny, between 1 and 2 inches in length. It looks like a tiny orange, with a thin, edible skin. The flesh is citrus-like in appearance and taste. Kumquats are often found crossed with other citrus fruits: limequat; lemonquat; orangequat; and the mandarin orange (calamondin).

- 2 pounds kumquats
- 1 tablespoon baking soda
- 1 1/2 pounds sugar
- 1 cinnamon stick
- 1/2 teaspoon ground cardamom
- 3/4 cup fresh Key lime, lime or lemon juice

1. Soak and rinse kumquats thoroughly. I like to use one of those vegetable-fruit washes for this.

2. Place kumquats in a large kettle or stock pot. Sprinkle with baking soda. Pour boiling water over top and allow to sit for 15 minutes.

3. Drain, return to kettle, fill with water, drain and rinse. Repeat three more times. Cut each kumquat in half. Return to kettle.

4. Add 5 cups of water to kettle, sugar, cinnamon stick, ground cardamom and lime juice. Return to boil and using a candy thermometer, make sure water temperature reaches 220°. Remove from heat and cover. Allow to sit for 30 minutes.

5. Transfer fruit to sterilized canning jars, following manufacturer's instructions. Discard cinnamon stick. Pour syrup to top of jar.

MANGO BUTTER

Region: Lower Florida, The Keys
Yield: about 1 quart

Serve as a spread over breakfast rolls, ice cream, pies or as a foil to a spicy fish, meat or chicken dish.

- 4 cups fresh diced mango
- 1 cup water
- 1/2 cup fresh Key lime, lime or lemon juice
- 2 1/4 cups sugar
- 1/2 teaspoon ground cardamom
- 1/4 teaspoon ground cinnamon

1. Cook mango in water and lime juice in a large saucepan over moderate heat for 10 minutes. Reduce heat, add sugar and continue to cook until a smooth puree, about 30 minutes and a candy thermometer reaches

220°. Stir in cardamom and cinnamon for the last five minutes of cooking.

2. Pour into sterilized canning jars and follow manufacture's instructions.

PAPAYA BUTTER

Region: Lower Florida, The Keys
Yield: about 1 pint

  2   cups fresh ripe papaya pulp
  1/2 cup fresh Key lime or lime juice
  1 1/2 cups sugar
  1/2 teaspoon almond extract

1. Place papaya in large saucepan and fill with just enough water to cover fruit. Bring to boil over medium heat, reduce heat and simmer for five minutes.

2. Stir in lime juice and sugar. Cook until a candy thermometer reads 220°. Remove from heat, and allow to cool for 30 minutes. Stir in almond extract.

3. Transfer to sterilized jars, following manufacturer's instructions.

GUAVA JELLY

Region: Central Florida
Yield: about 2 quarts

  2   pounds guavas
  1   cup fresh Key Lime, lime or lemon juice
  3   cups sugar
  1/2 teaspoon ground cardamom
  1/2 teaspoon orange extract

1. Peel and slice guavas. Place in a deep kettle and cover with just cold water to cover fruit. Bring to a boil, reduce heat to simmer, cover and cook for 1 1/2 hours. You should have 220° on a candy thermometer.

2. Remove from heat and cool.

3. Stir in lime juice, cardamom and sugar. Return to a low simmer, and cook until jelly stage is reached. Remove from heat, and cool for 10 minutes. Stir in orange extract.

4. Pour into sterilized jars and follow manufacturer's instructions.

HABAÑERO BARBECUE SAUCE

Region: Florida-Caribbean
Yield: about 2 to 3 cups

This sauce is for those who like it hot, and I do mean HOT, not just a little zesty. Habañeros or Scotch Bonnets are one of the hottest peppers on earth. Take extra care handling this pepper, not to put your finger in your eyes or other sensitive areas. Use for chicken, pork, beef and seafood.

- 1 tablespoon olive oil
- 1 large onion, finely chopped
- 4 garlic cloves, crushed
- 1/2 cup fresh Key lime or lemon juice
- 1/2 cup malt vinegar
- 1/2 cup water
- 1/4 cup packed brown sugar
- 1 (6-ounce) can tomato paste
- 1 tablespoon Worcestershire™ sauce
- 1 habañero pepper, seeded and finely chopped
- 1 teaspoon dry mustard
- 1 teaspoon salt
- 3 tablespoons dark rum
- 1/2 teaspoon dried thyme

1. Sauté the onion and garlic in the olive oil over moderate heat in a large saucepan until lightly browned.

2. Add lime juice, vinegar, water, brown sugar, tomato paste, Worcestershire™, habañero pepper, dry mustard and salt. Stir and bring to a boil.

3. Shut off heat. Add rum and thyme, stir and cover. Allow to sit for 20 minutes.

4. Pour into sterilized glass bottles. Keeps up to two weeks in the refrigerator.

KEY LIME AND PAPAYA SEED DRESSING

Region: Gulf Coast and Keys
Yield: about 1 cup

I eat a lot of papaya and always wondered what to do with the copious amount of tiny black seeds. Papaya seeds are peppery and good for digestive disturbances. I keep a small food processor on hand for small jobs such as grinding these seeds.

1/2 cup olive oil
1/4 cup fresh Key lime or lime juice
3 tablespoons red wine vinegar
2 tablespoons papaya seeds
1 small onion, chopped
1 large clove garlic crushed
1/2 teaspoon salt
1 teaspoon Italian herb seasoning

1. Combine olive oil, lime juice, vinegar, papaya seeds, onion, garlic, salt and Italian seasoning in a blender or small food processor.

2. Transfer to a clean glass bottle or jar. Keeps several weeks in the refrigerator.

GREEN DIP

Region: Northeast
Yield: about 1 1/2 cups

The original version of this tangy sauce came from the St. Augustine area and was used for seafood. Since then, it's found it's way as far south as the Keys, and works equally well on roast chicken.

1 thick slice French or Italian bread
3 tablespoons fresh Key lime, lime or lemon juice
2 tablespoons cider vinegar
1/2 cup chopped fresh parsley
1/4 cup chopped fresh cilantro
1/4 cup coarsely chopped onion
4 garlic cloves, crushed
4 anchovy fillets
6 pimento-stuffed olives, coarsely chopped
1 tablespoon capers
1/2 teaspoon sugar
1/4 teaspoon cayenne pepper

1. Remove the crust from the bread and discard. Tear bread into pieces.

2. Place bread pieces, lime juice, vinegar, parsley, cilantro, onion, garlic, anchovies, olives, capers, cayenne and sugar into a small food processor.

3. Puree until smooth. Transfer to a clean glass jar and refrigerate overnight to allow flavors to mingle.

Authentic Key Lime Pies and Key Lime Treats

FLORIDA WOULDN'T BE FLORIDA without Key Lime Pie. And, folks from the Keys are very particular about their Key Lime pies. If it doesn't contain Key limes (not the large Persian variety available in the grocer), it's not the real thing. Further, food coloring is never used—Key Lime Pie is a lemony yellow color because the juice of Key limes is yellow.

Key Lime Pie is made with sweetened condensed milk, which harkens back to the days before refrigeration, where this tinned milk became very popular in the southern United States, Caribbean, Cuba and South America. Fresh milk was not trucked into the Keys until the Overseas Highway was completed in the 1930's.

When you travel through the Keys, you will find dozens of signs, menus, restaurants, homes, bakeries advertising 'authentic' Key Lime Pie. Some versions have a meringue topping, others, whipped cream. Some cooks bake the pie briefly, others spoon the filling into baked pie crusts.

Older Key residents say their grandmothers used a flaky baked crust, like the kind used for apple pie. Today, many people use a graham cracker crust. Both are good.

My suggestion is to try as many Key limes pies as you can so you'll become an authority.

NOTE: Take care when using uncooked eggs as they may contain dangerous bacteria. I prefer to bake the pie, which cooks the eggs.

THE RECIPES

TRADITIONAL KEY LIME PIE WITH MERINGUE TOPPING

Region: Florida Keys
Yield: 8 servings

This good and basic recipe for Key Lime Pie is surprisingly short: beat 4 egg yolks, add sweetened condensed milk, then whisk in a half cup of lime juice.

- 4 extra large eggs, separated
- 1 cup (14-ounce can) sweetened condensed milk
- 1/2 cup fresh Key lime or lime juice
- 1 (9-inch) pie shell, baked and cooled
- 1/2 teaspoon cream of tartar
- 1/8 teaspoon salt
- 1/2 cup, less 1 tablespoon, sugar
- 1/2 teaspoon vanilla extract

1. Beat egg yolks in a medium bowl until thick and frothy. Drizzle in condensed milk and beat again until thick. Add lime juice and beat until thick.

2. Pour mixture into baked pie crust.

3. Preheat oven to 375º.

4. Beat remaining egg whites until soft peaks begin to form. Add cream of tartar, salt, vanilla, then slowly add sugar until stiff peaks form.

5. Spoon over lime filling. Bake until lightly golden, about five to six minutes. Allow to cool completely, about an hour and a half before refrigerating.

AUTHENTIC KEY LIME PIE

Yield: 8 servings

The difference between this recipe and the preceding one is that this one uses a graham cracker crust, instead of a flaky pie crust. The addition of lime zest adds a pleasing green tint to the filling.

LIME FILLING

- 1 tablespoon grated fresh lime rind
- 4 extra-large egg yolks
- 1 cup (14-ounce can) sweetened condensed milk
- 1/2 cup fresh Key lime or lime juice

KEY LIME PIE

Have you ever wondered how Key Lime Pie set without baking? It's because the acid content of the lime juice interacts with the proteins in the egg yolks and condensed milk—this is called clabbering.

GRAHAM CRACKER CRUST

- 12 graham crackers
- 3 tablespoons, plus 1 teaspoon granulated sugar
- 1/4 teaspoon ground cinnamon
- 5 tablespoons butter, melted
- 1/2 teaspoon almond extract

WHIPPED CREAM TOPPING

- 3/4 cup chilled heavy cream
- 3 tablespoons granulated sugar
- 1/2 teaspoon vanilla extract

FILLING

1. Beat lime rind into egg yolks with a hand mixer set on low in a medium bowl for two and a half minutes. The eggs will be tinted green. Whisk in condensed milk, then lime juice. Set aside. Do not refrigerate as filling will begin to thicken on its own.

CRUST

1. Place oven rack in center position, and preheat oven to 325ºF. Process graham crackers in a food processor until fine—you should have about a cup and a quarter. Sprinkle in sugar and cinnamon, combining well. Drizzle in butter and almond extract, stirring well. Press into a 9-inch pie pan, on bottom and sides. Bake until just browned, about 12 to 15 minutes. Cool on wire rack for 30 minutes.

FILLING PIE

1. Return oven to 325ºF. Spoon filling into crust and bake for 15 to 18 minutes. Filling will be firm, yet wiggly in center. Cool on wire rack for two hours. Refrigerate for several hours.

WHIPPED CREAM

1. Whip chilled cream in a medium bowl using a hand mixer until soft peaks form. Sprinkle in sugar and vanilla, beating for additional two minutes. Spoon over top of chilled pie.

FROZEN KEY LIME PIE

Yield: 2 pies, or 16 servings

1/2 cup fresh Key lime or lime juice
2 teaspoons grated fresh lime rind
1 teaspoon vanilla extract
1 cup sweetened condensed milk
1 (16-ounce) container slightly thawed frozen non-dairy whipped topping
a couple drops green food coloring
2 prepared graham cracker pie crusts

1. Beat together Key lime juice, lime rind, vanilla, condensed milk, and whipped topping until smooth. Divide equally between two pie crusts.

2. Place in freezer until firm. Serve frozen.

DARK CHOCOLATE KEY LIME PIE

Yield: 8 to 10 servings

3/4 cup grated dark chocolate or semi-sweet chocolate bits
1/4 cup, plus 2 tablespoons heavy cream
1/2 teaspoon almond extract
1/8 teaspoon cinnamon
1 (9-inch) pie shell, baked and cool
4 extra large eggs, separated
1 cup sweetened condensed milk
1/2 cup Key lime or lime juice
whipped cream
1/4 teaspoon cream of tartar
1/2 cup sugar
1/2 teaspoon vanilla extract
1 Key lime, cut in thin, almost transparent slices

1. Combine chocolate and heavy cream in a double boiler. Stir constantly until chocolate is melted and mixture is smooth. Whisk in almond extract and cinnamon.

2. Pour into bottom of pre-baked pie crust. Tilt and swirl chocolate to evenly coat bottom and sides. Chill in refrigerator.

3. Beat egg yolks in a medium bowl until thick and frothy. Drizzle in condensed milk and beat again until thick. Add lime juice and beat until thick.

4. Preheat oven to 325° F.

5. Pour lime filling into chocolate covered pie shell. Beat remaining egg whites with cream of tartar until soft peaks form. Beat in sugar and vanilla gradually.

6. Spoon on top of lime filling. Bake for 15 to 20 minutes until meringue is golden. Garnish meringue with lime slices. Chill in refrigerator.

KEY LIME CHEESECAKE

Yield: 10 servings

2 1/2 cups crushed graham crackers
1/2 teaspoon grated fresh ginger
1/2 cup butter, melted
2 (8-ounce packages) cream cheese, softened
1 1/2 cups sugar
5 large eggs, room temperature

5 teaspoons grated fresh lime rind
1/4 teaspoon almond extract
1 teaspoon vanilla extract
3/4 cup fresh Key lime or lime juice
9" inch spring form pan

FOR CRUST

1. Adjust oven rack to center position, and preheat oven to 325°F. Combine graham crumbs, ginger and melted butter in a medium bowl. Press on the bottom and sides of the spring form pan. Bake until lightly browned. Cool on wire rack.

FILLING

1. Beat cream cheese in bowl of electric mixer until smooth. Add sugar slowly until completely dissolved. Beat in eggs one at a time, on medium speed. Stop after the addition of each egg to scrape down sides of bowl. Whisk in almond extract, lime rind, almond and vanilla extract along with lime juice.

2. Pour batter into graham cracker crust. Bake at 300°F for 45 minutes. Cover top loosely with foil and bake additional 45 minutes. Shut off oven and leave cake inside for another hour.

3. Remove from oven, and cool completely in refrigerator. Serve when chilled.

LIMES

Limes come from a thorny tree native to the Far East, somewhere around India. Lime trees grow up to 14 feet in height, flowering year-round. This green citrus fruit came to France and Italy in the 13th century. In the 18th century, Scottish Naval surgeon Sir James Lind discovered that citrus fruit conquered scurvy (Vitamin C deficiency).

Key limes: Key limes were cultivated for thousands of years in the Indo-Malayan region. Columbus brought the fruit to Hispaniola, where in turn it traveled to Florida, particularly the Keys. Key limes are much smaller and thinner-skinned than Persian limes. Green Key limes are actually the immature fruit. Once the fruit has yellowed it is considered ripe.

Persian limes: This variety is believed to be a cross between a Mexican lime and a variety of lemon, called the citron. Carried from Persia to Brazil via Portuguese traders, it traveled to California in the late 1800's. Even though Florida is famous for its Key limes, it is the largest producer of Persian limes in the U.S.

Purchasing: Choose firm, but not rock hard, fruits heavy for their size. Do not buy dull or bruised fruits.

Storing: Keep at room temperature for a week. Keep away from bright light or they will lose their acidity. Store in refrigerator, unwrapped in a drawer for up to two weeks.

Nutritional info: High in Vitamin C, good in potassium, folic acid and some calcium.

CHOCOLATE KEY LIME CHEESECAKE

Yield: 8 to 10 servings

- 1 (8-ounce package) cream cheese, softened
- 1 (14-ounce) can sweetened condensed milk
- 1 teaspoon grated fresh lime rind
- 1/2 cup Key lime juice or lime juice
- 1 prepared chocolate graham cracker crust

1. Beat the cream cheese and the condensed milk with an electric hand beater until smooth and no lumps remain. Gradually add in Key lime juice and lime rind, blending until smooth.

2. Pour into chocolate graham cracker crust. Refrigerate until set.

KEY LIME CAKE

Yield: 8 servings

At one point I had tried so many different versions of Key Lime Pie, I began to worry my figure would suffer. So I began tasting Key Lime cakes instead, in the hope they were less fattening. This recipe was inspired by the many Key Lime cakes I tried.

CAKE

- 5 medium eggs, room temperature
- 1/2 cup whole milk, room temperature
- 1 tablespoon sweetened condensed milk, room temperature
- 1 1/2 teaspoons vanilla extract
- 2 cups cake flour, sifted
- 1 1/2 cups sugar
- 1/2 teaspoon ground ginger
- 2 teaspoons baking powder
- 1/2 teaspoon salt
- 1 cup (2 sticks) butter, softened
- 5 teaspoons grated fresh Key lime rind
- 1 tablespoon fresh Key lime or lime juice

GLAZE

- 1/2 cup fresh Key lime or lime juice
- 1 cup confectioner's sugar, sifted

CAKE

1. Adjust oven rack to lower-middle position. Preheat oven to 350ºF. Grease a 6-cup Bundt pan generously. Dust with flour and shake out excess.

2. Beat eggs, milks, and vanilla using a hand mixer set on low in a small bowl. Separate 1 cup of the egg mixture and set aside.

3. Sift cake flour again, along with sugar, ground ginger, baking powder and salt into the bowl of an electric mixer. Divide butter into half-inch chunks. Drop into flour mixture, one piece at time, with beater on low. Mixture will look like coarse sand.

4. Gradually beat in 1 cup of egg mixture. Beat on low speed for 10 seconds. Increase speed to medium and beat until fluffy about another minute. Whisk in remaining egg mixture, lime rind and 1 tablespoon of juice scraping down sides of bowl, about 30 seconds.

5. Spoon batter into the Bundt pan and bake for 20 minutes. Cover top loosely with foil and bake another 20 minutes. Cake is done when a toothpick inserted in center comes out clean, and cake begins to pull away from sides. Cool on wire rack for 12 minutes. Turn out onto rack.

GLAZE

1. Before the cake cools completely, beat together the confectioner's sugar and the Key lime juice until smooth. While cake is still warm, spoon glaze over top. Place a plate beneath rack to catch excess glaze. Reapply over top of cake until all glaze is absorbed.

KEY LIME CHEWIES

Yield: about 24 squares

- 1 cup raw almonds (unroasted kind can be found at health food store)
- 1 cup (2 sticks) butter, cut in pieces
- 2 cups all-purpose flour
- 1/2 teaspoon ground cardamom
- 1 teaspoon almond extract
- 4 jumbo eggs
- 1/2 cup sweetened condensed milk
- 1 cup granulated sugar
- 2 teaspoons grated fresh lime rind
- 3/4 cup fresh Key lime or lime juice

1. Preheat oven to 350º.

2. Grind almonds to a powder in a food processor. Add butter, flour, cardamom, almond extract and process until smooth. Press into an ungreased 13 x 9 x 2-inch glass-baking dish.

3. Bake for 15 minutes. Remove from oven.

4. Stir together eggs, condensed milk, sugar, lime rind, and Key lime juice. Spoon over almond crust. Return to 350º and bake for 30 minutes. Top should be set.

5. Cool and cut into squares.

KEY LIME COCONUT COOKIES

Yield: about 40 cookies

- 1 cup sweetened condensed milk
- 1/2 cup fresh Key lime or lime juice
- 1 teaspoon almond extract
- 1 teaspoon grated fresh lime rind
- 1/2 cup all-purpose flour
- 1/2 teaspoon ground cardamom
- 2 cups packed unsweetened unsweetened shredded coconut

1. Preheat oven to 350º. Generously grease two cookie sheets.

2. Whisk together condensed milk, lime juice, almond extract and lime rind. Sprinkle in flour and cardamom, mixing well. Fold in coconut.

3. Drop by spoonfuls onto baking sheet, leaving at least an inch and a half between cookies. Bake until golden, about 20 to 25 minutes. Cool on wire rack.

KEY LIME SORBET

Yield: 1 pint

Key limes make a wonderful sorbet and palette cleanser. Also, lovely after a heavy meal, where a different taste is called for, but not something too heavy.

- 1 cup sugar
- 1 1/2 cups water
- 1 teaspoon plain gelatin
- 1 cup fresh Key lime or lime juice
- 2 teaspoons grated fresh lime rind
- 2 tablespoons Cointreau™ (orange liqueur)

1. Combine the sugar and water in a medium saucepan over medium heat. Bring to a boil and stir occasionally until all sugar is dissolved and a full boil is attained. Remove from stove and stir in gelatin. Cool.

2. Stir in Key lime juice, lime rind and Cointreau™ into cooled syrup. Refrigerate until cold, then pour into ice-cream freezer, following manufacturer's instructions. Alternatively, place bowl in freezer, removing every few hours to beat. Serve within 24 hours and remove from freezer eight minutes before serving to soften and achieve peak flavor.

KEY LIME COOKIES

Yield: about 48 cookies

- 1 1/4 cups all-purpose flour
- 1 1/2 teaspoons cornstarch
- 1 teaspoon baking powder
- 1/2 teaspoon salt
- 1/4 teaspoon ground cardamom
- 1/2 (1 stick) cup butter, softened
- 1 teaspoon vanilla extract
- 2 egg yolks, beaten
- 3/4 cup sugar
- 2 tablespoons fresh Key lime or lime juice
- 1 tablespoon grated fresh lime rind

1. Preheat oven to 375ºF, and grease two cookie sheets.

2. Sift together flour, cornstarch, baking powder, salt and cardamom. Set aside.

3. Cream butter, vanilla, eggs, sugar, lime juice and rind in a large bowl until light and fluffy. Fold in dry ingredients until smooth and lump-free.

4. Drop by spoonfuls on cookie sheets, leaving at least one to two inches between cookies. Bake until golden, about 10 to 12 minutes.

KEY LIME FUDGE

Yield: about 2 pounds

- 2 (8-ounce) packages semisweet chocolate bits
- 1 can sweetened condensed milk
- 3 tablespoons fresh Key lime or lime juice
- 5 teaspoons grated fresh lime rind
- 1 teaspoon vanilla extract
- 1/4 teaspoon salt

1. Line an 8-inch square glass-baking dish with plastic wrap.

2. Heat chocolate and condensed milk in a double boiler, stirring constantly, until chocolate melts. Stir in Key lime juice, lime rind, vanilla and salt.

3. Remove from heat and pour into baking dish. Cool, then refrigerate until firm, at least two hours.

4. Lift fudge out of pan by plastic wrap. Cut into squares. Store in Datil covered container for up to two weeks in refrigerator.

Luscious Tropical Desserts

KEY LIME PIE is Florida's most famous dessert. But, you'll want to try this state's other goodies made from strawberries, papaya, banana, coconut, mango, oranges, grapefruit and assorted tropical fruits.

This chapter contains such traditional favorites such as flan and trés leches cake, both a must if you're preparing a Cuban meal. For the chocoholics, there are Chocolate and Macadamia Baked Bananas, Orange and Chocolate Turnovers and Rich Orange Fudge. Last, and most importantly, Chocolate Rum Cake.

THE RECIPES

Mango Banana Bread with Toasted Coconut Topping

Mango Ice Cream

Orange-Coconut Quick Bread

Orange Coconut Cream Cheese Tart

Rich Orange and Chocolate Fudge

Orange, Coconut and Chocolate Turnovers

Glazed Orange Almond Cookies

Piña Colada Cheesecake

Florida Orange Trés Leches Cake

Coconut Christmas Candy

Cuban Flan with Caramelized Mango Topping

Orange Cream Pie

Orange Peach Sherbet

Citrus Mini Tart with Grand Marnier Cream

Pineapple Layer Cake

Whipped Papaya with Rum and Lime

Peanut Butter Pie

Chocolate Rum Cake

CHOCOLATE AND MACADAMIA BAKED BANANAS

Region: Southern Florida
Yield: 4 servings

This rich dessert melts in your mouth. The ingredient list is delightfully short, yet the flavor, huge.

- 4 ripe, slightly green bananas
- 1 1/2 cups, semi-sweet chocolate bits
- 3/4 cup coarsely chopped macadamia nuts, lightly toasted under broiler for 10 minutes until golden
- 1/4 cup Amaretto™ liqueur
- 1/8 teaspoon ground cinnamon
- 1/2 teaspoon grated fresh lemon rind

1. Preheat oven to 375° F.

2. Wash outside of each banana thoroughly with soap and water.

3. Cut a slit in each banana, lengthwise. Bake in oven for 20 minutes. Remove from oven and fill with chocolate bits and macadamia nuts.

4. Combine liqueur, cinnamon and lemon rind in a cup. Drizzle over bananas.

5. Return to oven and bake until chocolate is melted. Serve hot.

STRAWBERRY PIE

Region: Southern Florida, Homestead
Yield: 8 servings

Until I moved to Florida, I had no idea the state grew strawberries in such an abundance. Fort some reason, I thought strawberries were a California thing. These fragrant berries are farmed near Homestead, and you'll find strawberry pie on many restaurant menus during berry season.

- 1 (9-inch) pie crust, baked
- 1 quart, or 3 pounds strawberries
- 3/4 cup sugar
- 1/2 teaspoon salt
- 1/2 cup water
- 3 tablespoons cornstarch
- 3 tablespoons fresh Key lime or lime juice
- 1/2 cup heavy cream
- 2 tablespoons sugar
- 1 tablespoon orange liqueur
- 1/2 teaspoon almond extract

1. Rinse berries under cool running water, then cut off stems. Reserve 1 cup of berries, and put remainder in refrigerator.

2. Mash the reserved cup berries with the salt, sugar and 3/4 cup water in a medium saucepan. Bring to boil and sprinkle in cornstarch. Stirring constantly, cook until mixture thickens.

Remove from heat and cool. Refrigerate for two hours.

3. Remove strawberry sauce from refrigerator and stir in lime juice. Arrange whole strawberries in pie shell and pour strawberry sauce over top. Refrigerate for at last one hour.

4. Just before serving, whip cream until soft peaks form. Sprinkle in sugar, orange liqueur and almond extract. Beat until stiff. Serve at once.

WARM STRAWBERRY BREAD

Region: Southern Florida, Homestead
Yield: 2 loaves

There's nothing quite so wonderful as strawberry bread. Strawberries are grown commercially in Florida.

3 1/4 cups all-purpose flour
2 teaspoons baking powder
1 teaspoon salt
1/2 teaspoon ground cinnamon
1/4 teaspoon ground cardamom
3/4 cup sugar
4 eggs, lightly beaten
1 cup vegetable oil
1/2 teaspoon almond extract
1/2 teaspoon vanilla extract
2 cups strawberries, hulled and sliced in half if large
2 teaspoons grated fresh lemon rind
1 1/2 cups chopped walnuts

1. Preheat oven to 375º F. Lightly grease and flour two 9 x 5 x 3-inch loaf pans.

2. Sift flour, baking powder, salt, cinnamon, and cardamom into a medium bowl. Whisk in sugar.

3. Combine eggs and vegetable oil in small bowl. Fold egg mixture, along with almond and vanilla extract, into flour until just combined. Incorporate strawberries, walnuts and lemon rind. Scrape batter into pans. Bake one hour, or until a toothpick inserted in center comes out clean.

STRAWBERRY ICE CREAM

Region: Southern Florida
Yield: about 1 1/2 quarts, 6 servings

There's nothing complicated about making old-fashioned ice cream. This classic, custard-based recipe is irresistible.

> 3 cups fresh strawberries, hulled and sliced
> 1 cup sugar
> 1 tablespoon orange liqueur
> 1/4 teaspoon salt
> 1 1/2 cups whole milk
> 1 cup heavy cream
> 4 tablespoons sweetened condensed milk
> 5 large egg yolks, beaten
> juice from 1 lime (1 tablespoon)
> 1 1/2 teaspoons vanilla extract
> 1/2 teaspoon almond extract
> 1 tablespoon vodka
> 1 tablespoon orange liqueur

1. Toss the strawberries with a half cup of the sugar, the salt and orange liqueur in a medium non-reactive saucepan. Macerate strawberries gently using a fork. Set aside.

2. Heat milk, cream, condensed milk and remaining half cup of the sugar in a medium saucepan, stirring occasionally, until the milk begins to steam, about five to six minutes.

3. Whisk egg yolks into the hot milk mixture. Cook over medium heat, stirring constantly until mixture steams again, and has slightly thickened. Do not boil or you'll have curdled egg drop soup. Remove from heat and strain into a heat-proof bowl. Stir occasionally to help the mixture cool.

4. Place sauce pan containing strawberries over medium heat. Simmer gently for three to four minutes. Remove from heat and transfer berries to a bowl. Whisk in lime juice, almond and vanilla extract as well as vodka and orange liqueur. Cool for thirty minutes, then stir into cooled milk mixture. Refrigerate for three to four hours.

5. Transfer strawberry custard to ice cream freezer, following manufacturer's instructions. Best if served within 48 hours.

BAKED BANANAS WITH RUM

Region: Southern Florida—Caribbean
Yield: 8 to 10 servings

Fast and easy!

   8 ripe, but firm, bananas
 1/2 cup lightly packed brown sugar
 1/2 teaspoon ground cinnamon
   3 tablespoons fresh Key lime or lime juice
 1/3 cup light rum
 1/2 teaspoon almond extract
 1/4 cup (1/2 stick butter), cut in
        1/4 inch slices

1. Lightly butter a 13 x 9 x 2-inch glass-baking dish. Preheat oven to 325°F. Peel bananas and slice in half lengthwise, and place face down in pan.

2. Combine brown sugar and cinnamon in a small bowl. Sprinkle over bananas.

3. Combine lime juice, almond extract and rum. Drizzle over bananas. Dot with butter. Cover with foil and bake for 30 to 40 minutes.

BANANA ICE CREAM

Yield: 1 1/2 quarts

   2 cups half-and-half, or light cream
   2 cups heavy cream
 3/4 cup sugar
   1 tablespoon light or gold rum
   2 teaspoons vanilla extract
 1/4 teaspoon salt
   6 ripe bananas, peeled and diced

1. Combine half-and-half, heavy cream, sugar, rum, vanilla and salt in a large bowl until sugar in completely dissolved.

2. Beat in banana chunks with an electric beater. Pour into ice-cream maker, and follow manufacturer's instructions.

3. Or, pour into a pan and place in freezer until slushy. Remove and beat with electric mixer and return to pan. Freeze until slushy. Repeat step three, twice more.

FLAMING CUBAN BANANA AND RUM TART

Region: Florida—Cuban
Yield: 8 servings

- 1 pie shell, baked and cooled
- 6 ripe bananas
- 1/2 cup sugar
- 1/4 cup lightly packed brown sugar
- 3 tablespoons butter
- 1/4 cup fresh Key lime or lime juice
- 1 teaspoon grated fresh lime rind
- 1/4 teaspoon salt
- 1/2 cup light rum
- 1 cup heavy cream, whipped into stiff peaks

1. Mash bananas in a medium saucepan. Stir in sugars and butter. Bring to a boil over medium heat, stirring constantly. Remove from heat.

2. Whisk in lime juice, lime rind and salt. Spoon into baked pie shell.

3. While filling is still warm, pour rum over top. Carefully light with a match. Serve with whipped cream.

KEY LIME COCONUT CHIFFON CAKE

Region: The Keys
Yield: 12 servings

Be sure egg whites are very stiff or the cake will fall.

CAKE

- 1 1/2 cups sugar
- 1 1/2 cups cake flour
- 2 teaspoons baking powder
- 1/2 teaspoon salt
- 6 large eggs (2 whole, 4 separated)
- 1/2 cup whole milk
- 1/2 cup butter, melted
- 5 teaspoons grated fresh lime rind
- 2 tablespoons fresh Key lime or lime juice
- 1 1/2 teaspoons vanilla extract
- 1/2 teaspoon cream of tartar

FLUFFY FROSTING

- 1 1/2 cups sugar
- 1/4 teaspoon salt
- 1/2 cup water
- 5 egg whites
- 1/2 teaspoon cream of tartar
- 1 teaspoon almond extract
- 1/2 teaspoon vanilla extract
- 1 cup packaged sweetened coconut flakes

CAKE

1. Adjust oven rack to lower middle position. Preheat oven to 325°F. Sift together sugar, flour, baking powder and salt in a large bowl. Set aside.

2. Combine 2 whole eggs, the 4 egg yolks, whole milk, melted butter, lime rind, lime juice and vanilla extract in a medium bowl until smooth. Fold into dry ingredients until just barely smooth.

3. Beat reserved egg whites in another good-sized bowl using an electric mixer on low speed until foamy. Increase speed to medium and sprinkle in cream of tartar. Beat whites until stiff, but not dry, about nine minutes.

4. Fold whites into batter, and pour into ungreased 9-inch Bundt pan. Tap pan against side of counter to rupture any air pockets.

5. Bake about one hour. Toothpick inserted in center will come out clean. Remove from oven and invert cake upside down over a glass bottle inserted through tube. Cool completely.

6. Invert cake onto plate for frosting.

FROSTING

1. Combine sugar, water and salt in a medium saucepan. Cook over moderate heat until mixture turns clear and temperature reaches 240°F on a candy thermometer, or until a small amount forms a soft ball when dropped into cold water.

2. Beat egg whites with cream of tartar and almond extract until stiff. Drizzle sugar syrup into egg whites and continue to beat.

TO ASSEMBLE CAKE

1. Spoon a generous amount frosting over top of one of the cakes. Place remaining cake on top of filling. Frost first the top, then the sides of cake with frosting. Press coconut flakes onto top and sides.

HOW TO CRACK AND GRATE A COCONUT

Coconut meat is delicious and superior in recipes to dried. First, look for coconuts without mold. Check the eyes, and be on the lookout for cracks. Choose coconuts that are heavy for their size.

Preheat oven to 400° F. Hammer through one of the eyes using a clean nail. Drain liquid and reserve for drinks and cooking. Bake coconut 15 minutes. Use a hammer to crack shell, and pry out meat with a sharp knife. Remove brown inside skin with a vegetable peeler. Grate by hand or through a food processor.

COCONUT POUND CAKE

Region: Northeast, St. Augustine
Yield: 10 servings

Traditional pound cakes do not use chemical leavening. Instead, they acquire their texture from eggs, and air incorporated while beating batter.

- 1 cup (2 sticks) butter, softened
- 1 1/4 cups sugar
- 3 large eggs, plus 4 yolks, room temperature
- 1 teaspoon vanilla extract
- 1/2 teaspoon almond extract
- 2 tablespoons light or gold rum
- 3/4 teaspoon salt
- 1 1/2 cups cake flour, sifted
- 2 cups grated fresh coconut, or 1 3/4 cups packaged unsweetened shredded coconut

1. Adjust oven rack to center position. Preheat oven to 325°F. Grease a 9 x 5 x 3-inch loaf pan. Line bottom of pan with parchment or waxed paper.

2. Whip butter in bowl of electric mixer at medium speed until shiny. Drop in sugar slowly, continuing to beat until light and fluffy, about five minutes.

3. Combine eggs, yolks, vanilla, almond extract and rum in a small bowl. Beating butter at medium setting, drizzle in egg mixture.

4. With beater still on, sift flour and salt into egg mixture a small amount at a time, until just combined. Do not over beat.

5. Fold in coconut by hand and turn batter into pan.

6. Bake until a toothpick inserted in center comes out clean, about seventy minutes. Rest cake for 15 minutes in pan, then invert onto wire rack. Remove waxed paper and flip cake right side up. Store at room temperature.

COCONUT PIE

Region: Southern Florida, The Keys
Yield: 8 servings

- 1 cup packaged sweetened coconut flakes
- 1/2 cup sugar
- 1/4 cup cornstarch
- 1/4 teaspoon salt
- 6 medium egg yolks, lightly beaten
- 1 1/2 cups whole milk
- 1 cup sweetened condensed milk
- 1 teaspoon vanilla extract
- 1/2 teaspoon almond extract
- 1/4 teaspoon ground cardamom
- 2 tablespoons butter
- 1 tablespoon light or gold rum
- 1 pre-baked 8 or 9-inch pie shell

1. Place oven rack to middle-lower position. Preheat oven to 300°F. Spread coconut in a thin layer in a pan. Bake, stirring now and then, until lightly browned. Remove from oven and set aside.

FILLING

1. Combine sugar, cornstarch and salt in a medium saucepan. Drop in yolks, then stir in whole milk and condensed milk. Cook over medium heat, stirring constantly, until mixture simmers and begins to thicken. Cook additional minute and a half, still stirring. Take pan off stove and whisk in vanilla and almond extracts, cardamom, butter and rum.

2. Fold in three-quarters of the toasted coconut and pour into heat-proof dish to cool. Press a sheet of plastic wrap directly over filling to keep a skin from forming. Cool for half an hour.

3. Scoop filling into baked pie shell and sprinkle with remaining coconut. Refrigerate thoroughly before serving.

COCONUT PUDDING

Region: Lake Okeechobee
Yield: 4 servings

- 1/2 cup sugar
- 1/4 cup cornstarch
- 1/4 teaspoon salt
- 5 large eggs, separated
- 1 3/4 cups whole milk
- 3/4 cup sweetened condensed milk
- 1 teaspoon vanilla extract
- 1/2 teaspoon lemon extract
- grated meat from 1 coconut (1 1/2 cups lightly packed)
- 1/8 teaspoon cream of tartar
- 2 tablespoons sugar

1. Whisk sugar, cornstarch and salt in a medium saucepan. Add egg yolks, then whisk in whole and condensed milk. Cook over medium heat, stirring constantly until mixture simmers and begins to thicken, about eight minutes. Continue to cook, stirring constantly for two more minutes.

2. Remove from heat, then stir in vanilla and lemon extract. Fold in coconut.

DID YOU KNOW?

Did you know that Florida has **7,700 lakes** greater than 10 acres?

3. Preheat oven to 325ºF. Pour into a greased square baking dish. Bake for 20 minutes. Remove from oven.

4. Beat egg whites, cream of tartar and 2 tablespoons sugar until stiff peaks form. Spoon over top of pudding and return to oven to brown.

COCONUT AMBROSIA

Region: Panhandle, Deep South
Yield: about 6 servings

Ambrosia is an important Christmas tradition in many Southern homes. I like to use Tupelo honey for this recipe. See resources for supplier.

> grated meat from 1 coconut (1 1/2 cups lightly packed)
> 4 to 5 medium assorted oranges, tangelos, grapefruit or other citrus, peeled, and cut in 1/2 -inch slices
> sugar
> 1/2 cup fresh Key lime or lime juice
> 6 tablespoons Tupelo honey (substitute regular honey)

1. Arrange a third of the coconut in a glass trifle, dessert or ambrosia bowl.

2. Place half the orange slices on the coconut.

3. Combine Key lime juice and Tupelo in a measuring cup. Drizzle 1/4 of dressing over orange slices.

4. Top oranges with another third of the coconut, then arrange remaining orange slices over coconut. Drizzle with another 1/2 cup of the dressing. Top with remaining coconut. Serve with extra dressing on side.

NOTE: You can substitute packaged unsweetened shredded coconut, but it won't be the same.

COCONUT SHERBET

The difference between sherbet and sorbet is that sherbet contains cream.

Region: Southern Florida
Yield: 4 servings

> 1 cup sugar
> 2 cups unsweetened coconut milk
> 4 tablespoons grated fresh coconut, toasted
> 3 tablespoons fresh Key lime or lime juice
> 1 tablespoon light rum
> 2/3 cup heavy cream

1. Dissolve sugar in 1/2 cup of the coconut milk in a medium saucepan over low heat. Simmer for 2 minutes. Remove from heat and cool for 15 minutes.

2. Stir in remaining coconut milk, Key lime juice and rum. When fully cooled, stir in cream.

3. Place in ice-cream freezer and follow manufacturer's instructions. Or, pour into a tray and place in freezer. When mixture becomes slushy, remove from tray and beat with an electric mixer for one minute. Return to tray and freezer. Repeat twice more. Serve topped with toasted coconut.

GRAPEFRUIT CREAM PIE WITH COCONUT CRUST

Region: Central Florida, Citrus Country
Yield: 8 servings

This recipe is similar to a Key Lime Pie, but uses grapefruit and lemon juice instead.

2 1/2 cups packaged unsweetened shredded coconut, or grated fresh coconut
1/2 cup (1 stick) butter, softened
1/2 cup packed brown sugar
1 teaspoon grated fresh lemon rind
1/4 teaspoon ground cardamom
4 large egg yolks, beaten
1/2 cup grapefruit juice
1/4 cup fresh lemon juice
1 teaspoon grated fresh lemon rind (if you use lime, the filling will turn green!)

1 (14-ounce) can sweetened condensed milk
1 grapefruit, sectioned, with membrane and seeds removed

1. Preheat oven to 400° F. Combine coconut, butter, brown sugar, lemon rind and cardamom in a small bowl. Press into the bottom and sides of a 9-inch pie plate. Bake for 10 minutes until golden. Remove from oven, cool and set aside.

2. Whisk egg yolks, grapefruit juice, lemon juice, 1 teaspoon lemon rind and condensed milk for two minutes. Set aside to thicken for 20 minutes.

3. Adjust oven to center position. Preheat oven to 325°F. Pour filling into pre-baked crust, rim edges of crust with foil to keep from burning, and bake for 15 minutes. Center will be set, but wiggly. Cool on wire rack to room temperature. Garnish with grapefruit segments in a pinwheel design. Refrigerate several hours.

LEMON BREAD PUDDING WITH MANGO LEMON POPPY SEED GLAZE

Region: Central Florida, Citrus Country
Yield: 6 to 8 servings

- 5 cups day old bread cubes
- 1/4 cup raisins
- 1/4 cup toasted walnut pieces
- 4 eggs, slightly beaten
- 2 cups whole milk
- 1 cup evaporated milk (not sweetened)
- 1/4 cup yogurt or sour cream
- 1/2 cup sugar
- 1 tablespoon grated fresh lemon rind
- 1/4 teaspoon ground cardamom
- 1 cup fresh diced mango
- 1/4 cup firmly packed brown sugar

GLAZE

- 1/2 cup confectioner's sugar
- juice of 1 fresh lemon
- 1/4 cup (1/2 stick) butter, softened
- 1/4 cup water
- 1 tablespoon poppy seeds

1. Preheat oven to 350° F. Toss bread cubes, raisins and walnuts in a large bowl. Arrange mixture on bottom of buttered 13 x 9 x 2-inch glass baking pan.

2. Combine eggs, whole milk, evaporated milk, sour cream, sugar, lemon peel and cardamom in a medium bowl. Pour over bread cubes.

3. Top with mango pieces. Sprinkle brown sugar evenly over top. Bake uncovered for one hour. Remove from oven.

GLAZE

1. Combine confectioner's sugar, lemon juice, butter, water and poppy seeds in a small saucepan over low to medium heat. Cook and stir until no lumps remain.

2. Serve over warm bread pudding.

LEMON AND SPICE CAKE TOP PUDDING

Region: Central Florida, Citrus Country
Yield: 6 to 8 servings

More soufflé than a pudding, nice after a heavy meal.

- 5 eggs, separated
- 1/2 teaspoon cream of tartar
- 1 cup granulated sugar
- 1/4 cup butter (1/2 stick)
- 2 tablespoons packed brown sugar
- 1/4 cup all-purpose flour

1/4 cup crushed raw almonds (run through food processor)

1 teaspoon almond extract

1/4 cup fresh lemon juice

1/4 teaspoon ground cardamom

1/4 teaspoon cinnamon

2 tablespoons grated fresh lemon rind

3/4 cup whole milk

1/4 cup evaporated milk

1. Beat egg whites with cream of tartar until soft peaks form. Beat in 3/4 cup sugar and 1/4 cup brown sugar for one minute. Set aside.

2. Beat egg yolks and butter. Gradually beat in remaining granulated sugar and brown sugar until light and fluffy, four to five minutes. Set aside.

3. Preheat oven to 325º F. Butter a 1 1/2 -quart baking dish. Set aside.

4. Mix together flour, crushed almonds, almond extract, lemon juice, cardamom and cinnamon. Beat in lemon rind, whole and evaporated milk. Carefully fold in egg whites.

5. Pour batter into prepared dish. Set dish inside a large dish, filled half-way with water. Bake uncovered for one hour until golden. Serve warm with whipped cream.

GINGERED LEMON SUNSHINE CAKE

Region: Panhandle, Deep South
Yield: 12 servings

Chocolate has always been my cake of choice. However, there's just something refreshing about a light and tangy lemon cake.

1 1/2 cups sifted cake flour

1 teaspoon baking powder

1/2 teaspoon baking soda

1/2 teaspoon salt

1/4 teaspoon ground cardamom

5 large eggs, separated

1/4 teaspoon cream of tartar

1 1/4 cups sugar

1/4 cup water

juice of one large lemon

1 tablespoon grated lemon rind

1 tablespoon grated fresh ginger

GLAZE

1 1/4 cups sifted confectioner's sugar

1/2 cup (1 stick) butter, softened

1/4 cup fresh lemon juice

1. Preheat oven to 350º F. Grease and flour a 9-inch Bundt pan. Sift together cake flour, baking powder, soda, salt and cardamom. Set aside.

CARDAMOM

Cardamom is the fruit of a ginger-family perennial native to India. The flavor is part lemon, part pepper, part vanilla, and just divine. Combines well with sugar and Tupelo honey in baked goods. I add it to all my pumpkin pie spice combinations. In the East cardamom is added to meats, fish, rice, as well as desserts and curries. Middle Easterners use it to flavor coffee. In Europe it's used to flavor deli meats, wines, and desserts.

Cardamom is reported to aid in digestion. In some parts of the world, people chew on cardamom seeds to freshen their breath. Cardamom is high in potassium, and also contains calcium.

2. Beat egg white and cream of tartar until soft peaks form. Gradually beat in 3 tablespoons of sugar until stiff. Set aside.

3. Beat egg yolks in a separate bowl until creamy. Beat in remaining sugar, water, lemon juice, lemon rind, and ginger.

4. Fold egg mixture into dry ingredients. Fold in egg whites. Spoon batter into Bundt pan.

5. Bake for 45 minutes until cake pulls away slightly from sides.

TO MAKE GLAZE

1. Beat confectioner's sugar, butter and lemon juice until smooth.

2. Place cake on plate, tucking strips of waxed paper to catch icing drips. Drizzle icing over cake. When dry, remove wax strips.

LEMON-CINNAMON ICE CREAM

Region: Central Florida, Citrus Country
Yield: 4 to 6 servings

    2 cups heavy cream
 1 1/4 cups sugar
  1/4 teaspoon ground cinnamon
  1/4 teaspoon ground cardamom
    2 tablespoons grated fresh lemon rind
  1/4 cup fresh lemon juice

1. Puree cream, sugar, cinnamon, cardamom, lemon rind and lemon juice in a blender until slightly thickened.

2. Pour into ice cube trays and freeze until nearly firm.

3. Whirl lemon cubes in blender or food processor until nearly smooth. Return to tray and freeze until nearly firm.

4. Puree in food processor again. Return to freezer in shallow pan.

5. Serve when firm.

MANGO TART WITH LIME-COINTREAU CUSTARD SAUCE

Region: Lower Florida, The Keys
Yield: 8 servings

This is my son Colby's all-time favorite pie. I advise doubling the recipe, and making two pies as it's sure to go quickly.

2 large, medium-ripe mangoes, peeled, and cut in 1/2 inch slices

CUSTARD TOPPING

1 2/3 cups whole milk
1 tablespoon grated fresh lime rind
1/4 teaspoon ground cardamom
5 egg yolks
1/4 cup, plus 1 teaspoon sugar
1/4 teaspoon salt
1 tablespoon Cointreau™ liqueur
1/2 teaspoon almond extract

DOUGH

2 1/2 cups all-purpose flour, plus extra for dusting
3/4 teaspoon salt
1 tablespoon, plus 1 teaspoon sugar
1 cup (2 sticks) firm butter, cut into 1/2 inch pieces

10 tablespoons solid vegetable shortening
6 to 10 tablespoons water

MANGO FILLING

1/2 cup sugar
1/4 cup packed brown sugar
1/2 teaspoon ground cinnamon
2 tablespoons light or gold rum
1/4 teaspoon orange extract
1 cup (2 sticks) firm butter, cut in chunks

1. Place mango slices in a colander to allow any excess juice to drain off. Reserve the juice to make tropical drinks.

TOPPING

1. Place milk and lime rind in the top of a double boiler, scalding milk. Combine cardamom, egg yolks, sugar and salt in a small bowl. Drizzle egg yolk mixture into hot milk, stirring constantly. Cook until mixture coats the back of a spoon. Remove from heat, and whisk in Cointreau™ and almond extract. Refrigerate until ready to serve.

DOUGH

1. Sift flour, salt and sugar into bowl of a food processor. Drop in pieces of butter and work into flour with short pulses or bursts from food processor. Add shortening, continuing with short bursts, until flour resembles pebbles or coarse sand.

3. Transfer mixture to medium bowl and add 6 tablespoons of water. Use a pastry cutter or two knives to cut water into flour. Add more water as needed to make dough come together into a smooth ball. Divide ball in two and flatten slightly. Dust with flour, wrap in plastic and refrigerate for one hour.

4. Lightly dust counter with flour. Place rolling pin in center of dough, apply light pressure and roll dough into a circle. To ensure that the crust will fit your pie plate, place the plate on top of the rolled out dough. The crust should extend two inches beyond the pie plate.

5. Fold dough in half, then in half again, so that it won't tear on its way to the pie plate. Place center corner of folded dough into middle of pie plate. Unfold dough, carefully tucking pastry into corners. Fold any dough overlapping the lip of the pie plate, beneath itself. Press down edges with the tines of a fork.

FILLING

1. Preheat oven to 350ºF. Arrange reserved mango slices along bottom of pie crust. Combine sugar, brown sugar, and cinnamon in a small bowl. Sprinkle over mango slices. Combine rum and orange extract, sprinkling over sugar mixture. Dot butter over sugar. Cover with foil and bake 35 minutes.

2. Remove foil, reduce heat to 300ºF and bake uncovered for additional 30 minutes to caramelize sugar and juices. Allow pie to cool for at 20 minutes. Spoon Lime-Cointreau Custard sauce over top.

MANGO-BANANA BREAD WITH TOASTED COCONUT TOPPING

Region: The Everglades
Yield: 8 servings

Believe it or not, I picked up this recipe in a casino snack bar smack in the middle of the Everglades. If you grease and flour only the bottom of a loaf pan, the bread will stick to the sides and rise taller.

1/2 cup packaged sweetened coconut flakes
 2 cups all-purpose flour
1/2 cup sugar
1/4 cup lightly packed brown sugar
3/4 teaspoon baking soda
1/2 teaspoon salt
 2 to 3 ripe bananas (mashed should equal 1 cup)
1/2 cup fresh diced mango
1/4 cup vanilla yogurt

2 large eggs, plus 1 white, beaten
1 tablespoon light rum
1/2 teaspoon vanilla extract
1/2 teaspoon almond extract

1. Preheat oven to 350°F. Spread coconut in a thin layer on a cookie sheet. Toast, stirring every couple minutes until golden. Remove from oven to cool.

2. Grease and flour bottom of a loaf pan. Sift together the flour, sugar, brown sugar, baking soda and salt into a medium bowl. Reserve.

3. Combine bananas, mango, yogurt, eggs, rum, vanilla and almond extract in a small bowl. Fold into flour mixture, until just combined. Mixture will look lumpy.

4. Spoon into loaf pan. Top with coconut. Bake for 55 minutes until a cake tester inserted in center comes out clean.

MANGO ICE CREAM

Region: The Keys
Yield: 2 quarts

1 1/4 cups sugar
1 cup heavy cream
4 cups fresh diced mango, juice and all

2 1/2 cups whole milk
1/4 cup sweetened condensed milk

1. Combine sugar and cream in a large bowl, stirring until sugar is dissolved. Fold in mango, whole milk and condensed milk.

2. Pour into an electric ice cream freezer and follow manufacturer's instructions. Or pour into a pan and set in freezer until mushy.

3. Remove from freezer and beat with an electric mixture, then return to freezer. Once mushy, repeat step three, twice more.

ORANGE-COCONUT QUICK BREAD

Region: Central Florida, Citrus Country
Yield: Makes 6 servings

Almost like an orange pound cake. Toast slices and serve with strawberry preserves.

1 large orange, unpeeled
1/2 cup fresh squeezed orange juice
2 tablespoons fresh Key lime or juice
2 1/2 cups all-purpose flour
2 1/2 teaspoons baking powder
1 1/4 teaspoons baking soda
1/2 teaspoon salt

1/2 teaspoon ground cinnamon

1/8 teaspoon ground nutmeg

1/8 teaspoon ground allspice

1/8 teaspoon ground cardamom

1 1/2 cups sugar

3 eggs

1/2 cup (1 stick) butter, softened

2 teaspoons grated fresh ginger

3/4 cup chopped walnuts

1/2 cup packaged unsweetened shredded coconut or fresh grated

1. Preheat oven to 350° F. Grease a 9 x 5 x 3-inch loaf pan.

2. Wash outside of orange with soap and water. Cut into 1-inch sections. Puree in blender with orange juice and lime juice. Mixture should have bits of orange peel visible.

3. Sift together flour, baking powder, baking soda, salt, cinnamon, nutmeg, allspice and cardamom. Set aside.

4. Beat eggs, sugar and butter in a large bowl until creamy. Stir dry ingredients into egg mixture, along with ginger until incorporated. Do not over beat.

5. Fold in walnuts and coconut.

6. Spoon batter into prepared pan. Bake for 55 to 60 minutes until a cake tester or toothpick comes out clean.

7. Cool on wire rack for 15 minutes. Remove from pan and continue to cool on wire rack. Nice served warm with a dollop of whipped cream.

ORANGE-COCONUT CREAM CHEESE TART

Region: Miami, Gold Coast
Yield: 6 to 8 servings

2 large oranges

1 (9-inch) pre-baked pie crust

1 egg white, slightly beaten

1/4 cup packaged unsweetened shredded coconut

2 (3-ounce) packages cream cheese, softened

3/4 cup confectioner's sugar

1 tablespoon Grand Marnier™ liqueur

1/4 teaspoon ground cinnamon

1 cup heavy cream

1. Preheat oven to 450° F. Grate 2 tablespoons rind from an orange and reserve its juice. Peel remaining orange and slice thinly in rounds. Place in colander and drain, reserving juice.

2. Brush pie crust with egg white. Press coconut into bottom and sides. Bake for 10 minutes. Remove from oven to cool.

3. Beat cream cheese, reserved juice, confectioner's sugar, Grand Marnier™, cinnamon and orange rind until smooth.

4. Whip cream in a separate bowl until stiff peaks form. Fold into cream cheese mixture, along with any drained orange juice.

5. Spoon into prepared pie crust. Arrange orange slices over cream cheese mixture.

6. Refrigerate four hours.

RICH ORANGE AND CHOCOLATE FUDGE

Region: Central Florida, Citrus Country
Yield: 12 servings

    2 cups granulated sugar
    2 tablespoons cocoa powder, sifted
  3/4 cup evaporated milk
    1 teaspoon vanilla extract
 11/4 cups semi-sweet chocolate bits
    2 tablespoons grated fresh orange rind
  1/4 cup (1/2 stick) butter, softened

1. Combine sugar, cocoa powder and evaporated milk in a double boiler over moderate heat. Stir constantly, bringing to a boil to dissolve sugar and cocoa powder into milk.

2. Reduce heat, add vanilla, and fold in chocolate bits and orange rind. Continue to stir until fudge thickens. Fold in butter.

3. Pour into buttered square baking dish. Refrigerate four hours. Cut into 1-inch squares.

ORANGE, COCONUT AND CHOCOLATE TURNOVERS

Region: Miami, Gold Coast
Yield: 4 servings

    1 large orange, peeled, sectioned, seeded and chopped
    1 tablespoon grated fresh orange rind
  3/4 cup semi-sweet chocolate bits
  1/2 cup packaged sweetened coconut flakes
  1/2 teaspoon almond extract
    4 puff pastry squares (about 5 to 6-inches)
    1 egg white, lightly beaten

1. Place orange pieces in a colander over a bowl to drain.

2. Combine orange pieces, orange rind, chocolate bits, flaked coconut and almond extract in a small bowl. Refrigerate.

3. Preheat oven to 350°F.

4. Place one puff pastry sheet on a piece of parchment or waxed paper. Brush lightly with egg white. Divide orange-chocolate filling evenly between all four pieces of pastry.

5. Fold over and press down firmly on edges with a fork.

6. Bake for 30 minutes until puffy and golden. Serve warm.

GLAZED ORANGE-ALMOND COOKIES

Region: Central Florida, Citrus Country
Yield: 24 to 36 cookies

These cookies remind me the scent of orange blossom filled orchards. Be sure to allow complete cooling or the icing will slide off the cookies.

1 1/2 cups all-purpose flour
  1/2 teaspoon baking powder
  1/2 teaspoon salt
  1/4 cup raw almonds, pulverized in food processor

3/4 cup (1 1/2 sticks) butter, softened
1/2 cup packed brown sugar
1/2 cup granulated sugar
1/2 teaspoon ground cardamom
  2 eggs
  1 teaspoon almond extract
1/2 teaspoon vanilla extract
  1 tablespoon grated fresh orange rind
  1 orange, peeled, seeded and chopped in food processor

GLAZE

  1 cup confectioner's sugar
  1 tablespoon Grand Marnier™ liqueur
  3 tablespoons butter, softened

1. Sift together flour, baking powder and salt. Fold in pulverized almonds. Set aside.

2. Cream together butter, brown sugar, granulated sugar, cardamom, eggs, almond and vanilla extract in a large bowl. Stir in chopped orange and

A Taste of Florida

rind. Slowly fold in dry ingredients until well blended. Cover and refrigerate for one hour.

3. Preheat oven to 375° F. Lightly grease 2 to 3 cookies sheets. Drop by tablespoonfuls on cookie sheets. Bake for 12 minutes until golden.

4. Cool completely on wire racks.
5. To make glaze: beat together confectioner's sugar, Grand Marnier™ and butter until smooth. Spread over cooled cookies.

PIÑA COLADA CHEESECAKE

Region: The Keys
Yield: 12 servings

COCONUT CRUST

   2 cups plain bread crumbs
  1/4 cup ground almonds
  1/2 teaspoon ground cinnamon
   1 cup packaged sweetened coconut flakes

  1/2 cup (1 stick) butter, melted
   1 teaspoon vanilla extract
   9 or 10-inch spring-form pan

FILLING

   2 (8-ounce packages) cream cheese, softened
  3/4 cup sugar
  1/2 cup cream of coconut (the sweetened kind used to make Piña Coladas, not coconut milk)
   4 large eggs, room temperature
   1 teaspoon grated fresh lime rind
  1/4 cup heavy cream
   3 tablespoons evaporated milk (unsweetened)
   3 tablespoons sour cream

TOPPING

   1 (20-ounce) can crushed pineapple
   4 tablespoons packed brown sugar
   1 tablespoon cornstarch (or use agar-agar found at the health food store)
  1/3 cup light or gold rum
  1/2 teaspoon vanilla
  1/2 teaspoon lemon extract

CRUST

1. Adjust oven rack to middle position. Preheat oven to 325ºF. Line bottom of spring-form pan with foil, wrapping extra foil beneath pan. Assemble pan.

2. Combine bread crumbs, ground almonds, cinnamon, coconut, butter and vanilla in a small bowl. Press onto bottom and sides of pan. Bake for 10 minutes and set aside to cool.

FILLING

1. Beat cream cheese with an electric mixer until smooth. Slowly add sugar and beat until sugar is dissolved, about three minutes. Incorporate cream of coconut. Add eggs one at time, until just mixed in, then add the next. Scrape down bowl sides after each egg. Stir in lime rind, heavy cream, evaporated milk and sour cream.

2. Pour filling into prepared pan. Bake 55 minutes at 325ºF, until sides pull away from pan, but center jiggles. Shut off oven, and using the handle of a wooden spoon to hold door ajar, keep in oven for an additional hour.

3. Remove from oven and set on wire rack to cool. Once at room temperature. Refrigerate for three to four hours. Keeps for several days in the refrigerator.

TOPPING

1. Heat the crushed pineapple, juice and all, sugar, and cornstarch in a saucepan over low heat, stirring constantly until boiling. Reduce heat, simmer until mixture thickens. Cool for 20 minutes and stir in rum, vanilla and lemon extract. Chill in refrigerator and spoon over top of cheesecake.

FLORIDA ORANGE TRÉS LECHES CAKE

Region: Florida, Cuba, Puerto Rico
Yield: 12 servings

1 1/2 cups all-purpose flour
1 teaspoon baking powder
1/2 cup (1 stick) butter
1 3/4 cups sugar
1/4 cup lightly packed brown sugar
6 large eggs, lightly beaten
2 teaspoons vanilla extract
3 tablespoons grated fresh orange rind
1 cup whole milk
3/4 cup evaporated milk
3/4 cup sweetened condensed milk
1/4 cup Grand Marnier™ (orange liqueur)
1 1/4 cups heavy cream

1. Preheat oven to 350ºF. Grease and flour a 13 x 9 x 2-inch baking pan.

2. Sift together flour and baking powder in a medium bowl. Set aside.

3. Cream butter, 3/4 cup sugar and 1/4 cup brown sugar until almost white in a separate bowl. Beat eggs in butter mixture until light and fluffy. Fold butter-egg mixture into flour mixture until smooth along with vanilla and orange rind, but not over beaten or cake will fall. Pour batter into prepared pan. Bake for 30 minutes or until a cake tester inserted in center comes out clean. Cool for 30 minutes.

4. Combine whole milk, evaporated milk, condensed milk and orange liqueur in a large measuring cup. Prick top of cake in a dozen places with a fork. Pour milk mixture over top of cake. Refrigerate for several hours or overnight.

5. Whip cream until soft peaks form. Gradually beat in remaining cup of sugar until stiff. Spoon over top of cake.

NOTE: You can substitute Cointreau™ for the Grand Marnier™. Cointreau™ is lighter in color and flavor than Grand Marnier™.

COCONUT CHRISTMAS CANDY

Region: Northeast, St. Augustine
Yield: about 1 1/2 pounds

Check out the index for instructions on grating coconut. Pay careful attention when making this traditional candy as it scorches quickly.

3 3/4 cups grated fresh coconut, reserving water from coconut
2 cups, plus 1 teaspoon sugar
1/4 teaspoon salt
1/2 cup, plus 2 tablespoons coconut water (liquid from inside a fresh coconut)
5 tablespoons corn syrup
1/2 teaspoon vanilla extract
1/2 teaspoon grated fresh lemon rind
scant pinch ground cardamom

1. Stir coconut, sugar, salt and coconut water together over medium heat in a large, light-colored saucepan. Keep stirring and bring to a boil. Do not burn or allow to turn dark in color.

2. Reduce heat, drizzle in corn syrup, vanilla extract, lemon rind, and cardamom. Stir until candy thickens, about 20 to 25 minutes. Do not take your eyes off pan or quit stirring, or mixture will brown.

3. To test for doneness, drop a teaspoonful on a piece of waxed paper. It should make a small mound that doesn't flatten, about 245° on a candy thermometer. Drop remaining candy by spoonfuls on waxed paper lined baking sheets. Cool completely, then store on waxed paper layers in airtight containers. Keeps up to one month.

CUBAN FLAN WITH CARAMELIZED MANGO TOPPING

Region: Miami—Cuban
Yield: 8 servings

Cuban rum is best for this recipe, but any good quality Caribbean rum will do.

butter for greasing
3/4 cup sugar
1 tablespoon water
8 eggs
8 tablespoons sugar
1/2 teaspoon salt
1 cup whole milk
1 1/2 cups evaporated milk
2 tablespoons light or gold rum
1 teaspoon vanilla extract

TOPPING
1 cup sugar
1/4 cup water
1 cup fresh diced mango with juice
2 tablespoons light or gold rum

1. Butter a 9-inch round cake pan. Place 3/4 cup sugar in a large heavy skillet and stir over medium heat until the sugar melts. Stir constantly so sugar does not burn. Carefully add water (it will splatter), cooking for an additional minute. Pour into cake pan. There's no need to tilt the pan to coat the sides, because when you invert the custard, the caramel will pour down the sides.

2. Preheat oven to 325°F. Make a hot water bath for the flan by setting the 9-inch pan inside a larger one filled with just enough water to cover three-quarters of the sides of the 9-inch pan, but making sure it doesn't float. Remove 9-inch pan, and set pan filled with water in oven.

3. Beat eggs with the eight tablespoons of sugar. Add salt, then whisk in whole milk, evaporated milk, rum and vanilla. Pour into 9-inch pan and set dish in pan filled with water. Bake an hour and a half, until a knife inserted in center comes out clean. Cool, then refrigerate overnight, or eight hours.

TOPPING

1. Cook sugar and water in a large heavy skillet over medium heat until golden and a syrup has formed. Stir constantly to avoid burning. Fold in mangos, coating with caramel. Stir in rum.

2. To turn out flan, loosen edge with a knife, place a plate with a lip over the pan, and flip quickly. Garnish with Caramelized Mango Topping.

ORANGE CREAM PIE

Region: Panhandle
Yield: 8 servings

1	package unflavored gelatin
1/2	teaspoon salt
3/4	cup sugar
3	large eggs, separated
1 1/4	cups orange juice
3	tablespoons grated orange rind
1/4	cup fresh Key lime or lime juice
1	teaspoon almond extract
1	cup heavy cream
1/4	teaspoon cream of tartar
1	orange, peeled and segmented
1	pre-baked 9-inch pie shell

1. Combine gelatin with salt and half the sugar in a medium saucepan. Set aside. Whisk egg yolks into orange juice in a large measuring cup. Stir into gelatin mixture. Cook, stirring constantly over low heat. Gelatin should be dissolved and mixture slightly thickened.

2. Remove from heat and whisk in orange rind, lime juice, and almond extract. Refrigerate two hours, stirring occasionally.

3. Whip cream until stiff. Set aside. Beat egg whites and cream of tartar for two minutes on medium speed. Sprinkle in remaining sugar gradually, beating until stiff. Fold into orange mixture. Fold in whipped cream.

4. Arrange orange segments along bottom of baked pie crust. Spoon in whipped orange mixture. Refrigerate for at least three hours.

ORANGE-PEACH SORBET

Region: Gulf Coast
Yield: 2 quarts

1 3/4 cups sugar
1/4 cup corn syrup
4 cups water
2 cups orange juice
1 tablespoon fresh grated orange rind
1 cup frozen or fresh peach slices, diced
1/4 cup fresh Key lime or lime juice

1. Combine sugar, corn syrup and water in a medium saucepan over moderate heat and bring to boil. Reduce heat, then stir in orange juice and orange rind. Cool for 20 minutes.

2. Stir in lime juice and diced peaches. Pour into electric ice cream freezer and follow manufacturer's instructions.

3. Or pour into a tray and place in freezer until slushy. Remove from freezer and beat with an electric mixture, return to tray and refreeze. Repeat step three twice more.

CITRUS MINI TART WITH GRAND MARNIER CREAM

Region: Central Florida, Citrus Country
Yield: 6 servings

1/4 cup fresh squeezed orange juice
1/4 cup Cointreau™ (orange liqueur)
2 tablespoons packed brown sugar
1/4 teaspoon ground cardamom
6 (3-inch) puff pastry rounds
12 sections of an orange
6 sections of a grapefruit (sliced in half if necessary)
1 cup heavy cream
2 tablespoons Grand Marnier™ liqueur

1. Combine orange juice, Cointreau™, brown sugar and cardamom in a small saucepan over moderate to high heat. Bring to boil, reduce heat, and cook down by half. You should have a syrup. Remove from heat and set aside to cool completely.

2. Preheat oven to 425º F. Place one tablespoon of syrup inside each puff pastry. Arrange the two orange sections and one grapefruit section

---

DID YOU KNOW?

The average winter temperature runs 53º F in Northern Florida, and 68.5º F in Southern Florida. Summer temperatures vary between 80.5º F (north) and 82.5º F (south). Hurricane season runs between June 1 and November 30.

A Taste of Florida

inside each pastry. Drizzle with additional syrup.

3. Bake for 10 to 12 minutes until golden. Remove from oven to cool slightly.

4. Beat cream until soft peaks form. Drizzle in Grand Marnier and continue to beat until stiff. Top each tart generously with whipped cream.

PINEAPPLE LAYER CAKE

Region: Lake Okeechobee
Yield: 12 servings

4	large eggs, room temperature
1/2	cup whole milk
1/4	cup evaporated milk
1	teaspoon vanilla extract
1	teaspoon lemon extract
2 1/2	cups cake flour, sifted
1 1/2	cups sugar
1	tablespoon packed brown sugar
2	teaspoons baking powder
1/2	teaspoon salt
1	cup (2 sticks) butter, softened, cut in 1/2 inch pieces

FILLING

1	tablespoon cornstarch
1/2	cup sugar
1	20-ounce can crushed pineapple
2	tablespoons light rum

FLUFFY FROSTING

1 1/2	cups sugar
1/2	teaspoon cream of tartar
1/4	teaspoon salt
1/2	cup water
5	egg whites
1	teaspoon almond extract

1. Place oven rack to lower-middle position. Preheat oven to 350°F. Grease two 9-inch cake pans. Cover bottoms of pans with wax or parchment paper. Grease waxed paper and dust entire pan with flour. Shake out excess.

2. Beat eggs, whole milk, evaporated milk, vanilla and lemon extract in a small bowl. Set aside.

3. Sift together flour, sugars, baking powder and salt into the bowl of an electric mixer. Add butter, 1 pat at a time with mixer running on low. Flour will look like coarse sand. Pour in 1 cup of egg mixture with mixer still running on low, about 10 seconds. Beat on high for one minute until fluffy. Slowly add remaining egg mixture, beating additional minute. Batter will look slightly curdled.

4. Divide batter equally between prepared pans. Bake until golden and a toothpick inserted in center comes

out clean—about 20 minutes. Cool on wire rack for 15 minutes. Run a knife around edges of cake, and flip over onto plate. Remove waxed paper. Cool before frosting, or icing will melt off cake.

FILLING

1. Combine cornstarch and sugar in a medium saucepan. Add a small amount of syrup from canned pineapple to pan, and stir until no lumps remain. Cook over moderate heat for two minutes, then fold in pineapple, cooking until mixture thickens. Remove from heat and cool. Stir in rum. Reserve.

FROSTING

1. Combine sugar, cream of tartar, water and salt in a medium saucepan. Cook over moderate heat until mixture turns clear and temperature reaches 240ºF on a candy thermometer, or until a small amount forms a soft ball when dropped into cold water.

2. Beat egg whites until stiff peaks form, but not dry. With the mixer running, slowly drizzle in sugar syrup. Continue to beat, adding almond extract, until stiff peaks form and frosting is cool and ready to spread.

TO ASSEMBLE CAKE

1. Spoon a generous amount of pineapple filling over top of one of the cakes. Place remaining cake on top of filling. Frost first the top, then the sides of cake with frosting. Serve any extra filing on the side with the cake slices.

WHIPPED PAPAYA WITH RUM AND LIME

Region: The Keys
Yield: 4 servings

2 cups fresh ripe papaya pulp
2 teaspoons grated fresh lime rind
1/4 cup fresh Key lime or lime juice
1/4 cup sugar
1/4 cup lightly packed brown sugar
4 egg whites, beaten until stiff
1 cup heavy cream
2 tablespoons sugar
2 tablespoons light or gold rum

1. Combine papaya, lime juice, lime rind and sugars in a food processor until smooth.

2. Fold in egg whites until just incorporated. Spoon into glass serving bowl or trifle dish.

3. Whip cream until light peaks form. Gradually beat in sugar and rum. Spoon over papaya.

NOTE: Recipe uses raw eggs, which may contain dangerous bacteria.

PEANUT BUTTER PIE

Region: Panhandle, Northern Florida
Yield: 12 servings

Peanut Butter Pie is to Northern Florida as Key Lime Pie is to the Keys. It's very rich. Serve in thin slices with hot coffee.

  1   (9-inch) pie shell, baked
  3/4   cup confectioner's sugar
  1/2   cup chunky or smooth peanut butter
  4   egg yolks, beaten
  1/2   cup granulated sugar
  1   teaspoon salt
  1/4   cup cornstarch
  1 1/2   cups whole milk
  1/2   cup evaporated milk
  1   teaspoon vanilla extract
  1   tablespoon butter
  1/4   teaspoon ground cinnamon
  1/4   teaspoon ground cardamom
  1   cup heavy cream
  semi-sweet chocolate shavings

1. Combine confectioner's sugar and peanut butter in a small bowl, and reserve. Mixture will be pebbly.

2. Beat egg yolks in top of double boiler. Whisk in sugar and salt, beating until fluffy. Sprinkle in cornstarch, beating constantly. Drizzle milks in a slow stream. Cook over moderate heat, stirring constantly, until thickened. Remove from heat. Fold in vanilla, butter, cinnamon and cardamom.

3. Sprinkle peanut butter crumbs into the bottom of the pie shell, reserving a couple tablespoons. Spoon custard over peanut butter crumbs.

4. Whip cream until stiff peaks form. Spoon over custard. Top with remaining peanut butter crumbs. Garnish with chocolate shavings. Chill for 2 hours before serving.

CHOCOLATE RUM CAKE

Yield: 12 servings

This is my most requested rum cake recipe. It's moist, dense, fudgy and floating in 151 proof rum. You know, I'm not a rum drinker, but something magical happens when you cook with it, in particular, baked goods.

chocolate baking powder (Hershey's)

1 package chocolate cake mix
1 package instant chocolate pudding mix
5 eggs, beaten
1/2 cup vegetable oil
1/2 cup water
1/4 cup light or gold rum
1 cup semi-sweet chocolate bits
1/2 cup 151-proof rum

1. Preheat oven to 325° F. Grease a Bundt pan and dust with cocoa powder.

2. Beat together cake mix, pudding mix, eggs, oil, water and rum for two minutes on high speed. Do not over beat as cake will fall apart. Fold in chocolate bits. Spoon into prepared pan.

3. Bake for 55 to 60 minutes. Remove from oven and cool on wire rack for 10 minutes. Poke holes into cake randomly. Pour 151-rum over top while still warm.

NOTE: This cake tastes better after a few days of 'soaking' in rum. Keep in sealed plastic or tin cake box.

Drinks

FLORIDA GETS HOT IN THE SUMMER, a fact that makes the locals parched. The snowbirds don't deal with the heat too well either, and they work up a powerful thirst. As a result, Florida has more than its share of watering holes, bars, and bistros.

Luscious tropical fruits combine well with Caribbean rum, vodka, exotic liqueurs and other libations. Don't be afraid to substitute. If you don't have orange-flavored vodka, try plain vodka or lemon vodka. If you don't have Crème de Cassis (black currant liqueur) use cranberry or cherry brandy. Bols™ makes a number of inexpensive, yet high-quality liqueurs. Who knows? You may come up with a delicious new drink recipe.

As always, take care while under the influence of alcohol. Do not drink and drive, ever.

LIQUEUR DEFINITIONS AND SUBSTITUTIONS

A number of the tropical drink recipes in this chapter use brandies and liqueurs. I've listed the descriptions of most of them, along with a number of substitutions. Some of the swaps work better than others; a few of the liqueurs really don't have a replacement.

— BERRIES

Boggs Cranberry Liqueur: cranberry; *substitute* cherry brandy
Blackberry brandy: *substitute* any other cranberry, cherry or berry liqueur or brandy.
Chambord: black raspberry, various fruits and botanicals, purple in color. Lovely floated on top of a wine spritzer or champagne; *substitute* any blackberry, cranberry, cherry brandy or liqueur, sloe gin.
Cherry brandy: *substitute* any other berry liqueur or brandy.
Crème de Cassis: French black currant, various fruits and berries; *substitute* cranberry, raspberry, blackberry brandy or liqueur or sloe gin.
Framboise or Fraise: strawberry brandy; *substitute* cranberry or cherry brandy
Kirsch: cherry brandy; *substitute* cranberry, raspberry brandy or liqueur or sloe gin.
Sloe gin: made from the sloeberry, a small purple plum and a bit of gin; *substitute* cranberry, black raspberry, cherry, strawberry brandy or liqueur.

— CHOCOLATE

Crème de Cacao: chocolate-flavored liqueur, available in clear or dark brown. Blend of vanilla and cacao beans.

— COFFEE

Kahlua: coffee-flavored liqueur made in Mexico with a hint of chocolate; *substitute* Tía Maria or any other coffee liqueur.
Nassau Royal: strong citrus flavor with a touch of coffee
Tía Maria: made from Jamaican Blue Mountain coffee, rum and spices; *substitute* Kahlua or any other coffee-liqueur.

— CREAM

Bailey's Irish Cream Liqueur: cream, Irish whiskey and other ingredients; *substitute* rum cream liqueur or equal parts whiskey and cream, with a touch of vanilla, sugar and a few granules of instant coffee.

Carolan's: another good Irish cream liqueur.

Cruzan Rum Cream: similar to Irish cream liqueur, except uses rum.

O'Darby's: another good Irish cream liqueur.

— FRUITS

Cointreau: orange liqueur made in France, which is a blend of sweet and bitter oranges nearly clear in color. Good for flavoring baked goods as well; *substitute* Triple Sec, Curacao, Tuaca or Grand Marnier, although the latter is heavier than the former.

Curacao, Blue or Orange: made from bitter oranges grown on the Caribbean island of Curacao. Be sure to use the blue color when specified in a drink. Of interest is that the Curacao which is made on the Caribbean island tastes different from that available on the U.S. mainland. I discovered this while on a cruise to the island where my son and I visited the distillery.

Grand Marnier: oranges and cognac, deep orange in color.

Midori or melon liqueur: made from green honeydew melons.

Orange liqueur: Grand Marnier, Cointreau, Curacao, Triple Sec.

Peach schnapps: peach brandy; *substitute* any peach brandy.

Persico: peach liqueur made by Bols with hints of almond and other tropical fruits.

Poire Williams: clear spirit made from Williams or Bartlett pears; *substitute* any apple brandy or peach brandy.

Southern Comfort: peaches, herbs, brandy and bourbon. I don't know if there is a substitute. Originally made by the Cruzan Rum Distillery on St. Croix in the U.S. Virgin Islands.

Tuaca: oranges and other herbs blended with brandy native to Tuscany, Italy; *substitute* any other orange liqueur.

— HERBS AND SPICES

B & B: Benedictine and cognac

Benedictine: contains over 27 herbs, botanicals and spices, including cloves, nutmeg, cardamom, myrrh and vanilla in a cognac base.

Chartreuse: an herbal liqueur made by Carthusian monks near Grenoble since the 17th century.

Galliano: sweet, bright yellow Italian liqueur flavored with over 30 herbs, including vanilla, juniper, yarrow, musk, anise and lavender, which comes in a tall, narrow bottle.

Parfait Amour: violet-flavored liqueur

— NUTS

Amaretto: almond-flavored liqueur made in Italy from apricot pits and herbs; *substitute* almond or hazelnut liqueur.

Frangelico: hazelnuts, berries and flowers; *substitute* almond liqueur such as Crème de Noyaux.

Liquor 43: vanilla-flavored liqueur, popular in Puerto Rico.

— MISCELLANEOUS

Coco Lopez™: very thick liquid made from grated coconut meat and sugar; *substitute* cream of coconut.

Rose's™ lime juice: sweetened concentrated lime juice,

Grenadine: also by Rose's™, a strong sweet red syrup made from red currants and pomegranates.

BANANA BALM

Yield: 1 serving

1 1/2 ounces vodka
 1/2 ounce banana liqueur
   splash of pear brandy
   1 teaspoon Rose's™ lime juice

1. Fill a cocktail shaker with ice. Add all ingredients, shake and strain into a rocks glass.

BANANA BOAT

Yield: 1 serving

 1/2 ounce coconut rum
 1/2 ounce banana liqueur
   splash of white Crème de Cacao (clear chocolate-flavored liqueur)
   splash of pineapple juice

1. Fill a cocktail shaker with ice. Add all ingredients, shake and strain into a shot glass.

BANANA DAIQUIRI

Yield: 1 serving

   2 ounces light or gold rum
 1/2 ounce banana liqueur

   splash of Rose's™ lime juice
   1 ripe banana, peeled
   1 cup of crushed ice

1. Combine all ingredients in a blender. Pour into a tall glass.

BANANA ISLAND

Yield: 1 serving

1 1/2 ounces vodka
 1/2 ounce banana liqueur
   splash of Rose's™ lime juice
   cream soda
   scoop of vanilla ice cream

1. Scoop vanilla ice cream into a hurricane glass. Pour vodka and banana liqueur over ice cream. Add splash of Rose's lime juice. Slowly fill to top with cream soda.

BEACH BUM

Yield: 1 serving

NOTE: Instead of using raspberry vodka, substitute regular vodka with a splash of cherry brandy.

- 1 ounce vodka
- 1 ounce Absolut™ Raspberry Vodka
- 1 ounce melon-flavored liqueur

1. Fill a cocktail shaker with ice. Add all ingredients, shake and strain into a martini glass.

BELLINI

Yield: 1 serving

- 1 ounce peach schnapps
- splash of apricot liqueur
- champagne

1. Pour the schnapps and liqueur into a champagne glass. Fill to top with champagne.

BARBARY COAST

Yield: 1 serving

- 1 ounce white Crème de Cacao
- 1/2 ounce Irish whiskey
- 1/2 ounce light rum
- 1/2 ounce gin
- 1 ounce light cream

1. Fill a cocktail shaker with ice. Add all ingredients, shake and strain into a rocks glass.

BERMUDA COCKTAIL

Yield: 1 serving

- 2 ounces gin
- 1 ounce apricot brandy
- splash of almond liqueur
- splash of cherry brandy
- 1/2 ounce fresh lime juice

1. Fill a cocktail shaker with ice. Add all ingredients, shake and strain into a martini glass.

BLACK ORCHID

- 1 1/2 ounces vodka
- 1/2 ounce Blue Curacao™
- splash of cherry liqueur
- 2 ounces cranberry juice cocktail

1. Fill a cocktail shaker with ice. Add all ingredients, shake and strain into a rocks glass.

BLUE LAGOON

Yield: 1 serving

1 1/2 ounces vodka
1/2 ounce Blue Curacao™
1/2 ounce orange liqueur
1 ounce fresh lemon juice
Club soda
Maraschino cherry for garnish

1. Shake all ingredients except club soda and cherry in a cocktail shaker filled with ice. Strain into a rocks glass. Top with cherry.

BLUE OCEAN MARTINI

Yield: 1 serving

1 1/2 ounces vodka
1 1/2 ounces tequila
splash of Blue Curacao™
lime wedge
salt

1. Wet the lip of a margarita glass with water or lime juice. Twist in a plate of salt. Shake all other ingredients in a cocktail shaker filled with ice, except lime. Strain into a margarita glass. Squeeze lime wedge into drink, and drop in.

BUSHWHACKER

Yield: 1 serving

1 ounce dark rum
1 ounce Irish cream liqueur
1/2 ounce dark Crème de Cacao (chocolate liqueur)
1/2 ounce coffee-flavored brandy
splash of almond liqueur
ground nutmeg
1/2 cup crushed ice

1. Combine all ingredients except nutmeg in a blender. Pour into a hurricane glass. Garnish with ground nutmeg.

CAPTAIN TONY'S HEAD BASHER

Yield: 1 serving

When I came across this drink in Key West, I thought I recognized it. Pusser's Restaurant in Tortola and Soggy Dollar Bar in Jost Van Dyke, both in the British Virgin Islands, concoct a similar drink called a "Painkiller." In case you're wondering, there is no dock at Soggy Dollar Bar. Patrons dive in warm Caribbean water and swim to shore. Hence, the name, Soggy Dollar Bar.

    3 ounces '151' proof rum
    1 ounce dark rum
    1 ounce pineapple juice
    1 ounce orange juice
    1 ounce grapefruit juice
    1 ounce Coco Lopez™ (cream of coconut)

1. Fill a cocktail shaker with ice. Add drink ingredients, shake and strain into a cocktail glass. In the islands, ground nutmeg tops this drink.

CARIBBEAN SUNSET

Yield: 1 serving

Key West is famous for its sunset parties at Mallory Square.

    2 ounces tequila
    1 ounce fresh Key lime or lime juice (don't worry; the juice is yellow, not green!)
    1 ounce orange juice
    1 ounce Grenadine syrup

1. Fill a rocks glass with ice. Pour the ingredients in the order shown, being careful not to disturb each layer. Garnish with an orange slice or lime wedge.

COCONUT CREAM PIE

Yield: 1 shot

1 1/2 ounces coconut rum
    whipped cream
    packaged sweetened coconut flakes

1. Pour coconut rum into a shot glass. Top with whipped cram. Sprinkle with coconut flakes.

COCONUT DREAM PIE

Yield: 1 serving

    2 ounce coconut rum
    1 ounce plain or citrus-flavored vodka
    splash of Irish cream liqueur
    2 ounces heavy cream
    1/2 cup crushed ice
    packaged unsweetened shredded coconut

1. Whirl all ingredients in blender except dried coconut. Pour into a hurricane glass. Garnish with coconut.

CREAMSICKLE

Yield: 1 serving

    1 ounce Galliano™ liqueur
    1/2 ounce plain or orange-flavored vodka
    1/2 ounce Irish cream liqueur
    splash orange juice

1. Fill a cocktail shaker with ice. Add all ingredients, shake and strain into a rocks glass.

CUBAN EL PRESIDENTE

Yield: 1 serving

    2 ounces light or gold rum
    1/2 ounce vermouth
    splash of Blue Curacao™
    1 ounce fresh lime juice
    splash of Grenadine syrup
    1 twist of orange rind
    cinnamon stick

1. Fill a cocktail shaker with ice. Combine all ingredients except orange twist and cinnamon stick. Strain into a rocks glass. Garnish with orange twist and cinnamon stick.

FLORIDA RUM RUNNER

Yield: 1 large serving

    1 1/2 ounces light or gold rum
    1 ounce banana liqueur
    1 ounce blackberry liqueur
    2 ounces fresh lime juice
    splash of Grenadine syrup
    1/2 cup crushed ice

1. Combine all ingredients in blender until smooth.

FUDGESICLE

Yield: 1 shot

NOTE: You can substitute plain vodka, but add a 1/4 teaspoon vanilla extract.

  1 ounce Stoli™ Vanil (vanilla) vodka
1/2 ounce dark Crème de Cacao
  splash cream

1. Fill a cocktail shaker with ice. Add all ingredients, shake and strain into a shot glass.

FUZZY NAVEL

Yield: 1 serving

1 1/2 ounces peach schnapps
  splash of Southern Comfort™
  orange juice

1. Fill a rocks glass with ice. Pour in schnapps and Southern Comfort. Stir in orange juice.

GRAPEFRUIT COCKTAIL

Yield: 1 serving

  2 ounces gin
  splash of cherry liqueur

  1 ounce grapefruit juice
  drop of Grenadine
  Maraschino cherry

1. Fill a cocktail shaker with ice. Add all ingredients, shake and strain into a martini glass. Garnish with a cherry.

IGUANA

Yield: 1 shot

1/2 ounce gold tequila
1/2 ounce coffee-flavored brandy
1/2 ounce plain or citrus-flavored vodka

1. Fill a cocktail shaker with ice. Add all ingredients, shake and strain into a shot glass.

IL PARADISO

Yield: 1 serving

  1 ounce Tuaca™
  1 ounce Blue Curacao™
  splash of Galliano™
  2 ounces whole milk

1. Fill a cocktail shaker with ice. Add all ingredients, shake and strain into a rocks glass.

JUICY FRUIT

Yield: 1 serving

1/2 ounce vodka
1/2 ounce melon liqueur
1/2 ounce peach schnapps
1/2 ounce banana liqueur
splash of pineapple juice

1. Fill a cocktail shaker with ice. Add all ingredients, shake and strain into a shot glass.

JUNGLE JIM

Yield: 1 serving

1 ounce vodka
1 ounce banana liqueur
1 ounce cream
splash of Frangelico™, or any other liqueur made from nuts

1. Fill a cocktail shaker with ice. Add all ingredients, shake and strain into a martini glass.

KEY LIME PIE COCKTAIL

Yield: 1 serving

2 ounces Liquor 43™ (vanilla flavored liqueur) or almond liqueur
1/2 ounce fresh lime juice
1/2 ounce Rose's™ lime juice
2 ounces heavy cream
1 cup crushed ice
lime wedge

1. Whirl all ingredients except lime wedge in a blender. Pour into a hurricane glass. Garnish with lime.

LA BOMBA

Yield: 1 drink

1 1/2 ounces tequila
  1/2 ounce Galliano™
   2 ounces orange juice
   2 ounces pineapple juice
splash of Grenadine

1. Fill rocks glass with ice. Stir all ingredients.

LATIN LOVER

Yield: 1 shot

1 1/2 ounces tequila
  1/2 ounce Amaretto™
  1/2 ounce Tuaca™

1. Fill a cocktail shaker with ice. Add all ingredients, shake and strain into a shot glass.

LEMON DROP

Yield: 1 shot

  1 ounce vodka or citrus-flavored vodka
splash of orange liqueur
lemon slice
sugar

1. Wet the rim of a shot glass and twist in a plate of sugar. Pour in vodka. Hand the drinker a lemon slice to suck on after doing the shot.

M & M

Yield: 1 serving

 splash of Grenadine
  1/2 ounce almond liqueur
  1/2 ounce coffee-flavored brandy

1. Layer ingredients shown into a shot glass.

MANGO CRUSH

Yield: 1 serving

1 1/2 ounces vodka
   1 ounce Mango rum
splash cherry brandy or Boggs™
   Cranberry liqueur

1. Fill a cocktail shaker with ice. Add all ingredients, shake and strain into a shooter glass.

MANGO MARGARITA

Yield: 1 serving

  2 ounces tequila
1/2 cup fresh or frozen mango chunks
  2 ounces fresh lime juice
splash of Triple Sec™
1/2 cup crushed ice

1. Whirl all ingredients in a blender. Pour into a margarita glass rimmed with salt or sugar.

MANGO SURPRISE

Yield: 1 serving

  1 ounce light rum
  1 ounce almond liqueur
1/2 ounce orange liqueur
1/2 cup fresh or frozen mango chunks
  2 ounces orange juice
  1 ounce heavy cream
1/2 cup crushed ice

1. Combine all ingredients in a blender. Pour into a hurricane glass. Garnish with orange slice.

MIAMI BEACH

Yield: 1 serving

1 1/2 ounces Scotch
1/2 ounce dry vermouth
  1 ounce grapefruit juice

1. Fill a low-ball glass with ice. Stir in all ingredients.

MIAMI ICE

Yield: 1 serving

1/2 ounce vodka or orange-flavored vodka
1/2 ounce gin
1/2 ounce white rum
1/2 ounce peach schnapps
  1 ounce orange juice.

1. Fill a rocks glass with ice. Stir in all ingredients.

MIAMI MELONI

Yield: 1 serving

1 ounce light rum
1 ounce melon liqueur

1 ounce cream
splash of Irish Cream liqueur

1. Fill a low-ball glass with ice. Stir in all ingredients.

MORE SUNSHINE

Yield: 1 serving

1 ounce gin
1 ounce cherry liqueur or Crème de Cassis
splash Galliano™
orange juice

1. Fill a rocks glass with ice. Stir in gin and Crème de Cassis. Fill to top with orange juice and float Galliano on top.

MUDSLIDE

Yield: 1 serving

1 ounce vodka or vanilla-flavored vodka
1/2 ounce coffee-flavored brandy
1/2 ounce Irish cream liqueur
cola

1. Fill a rocks glass with ice. Stir in first three ingredients. Fill to top with cola. Garnish with an orange twist. Be sure to twist rind first over drink for that precious drop of orange oil.

ORANGE BANG

Yield: 1 serving

1 1/2 ounce gin
1/2 ounce Tuaca™
splash Triple Sec
2 ounces orange juice

1. Shake all ingredients except orange slice in a cocktail shaker filled with ice. Strain into a martini glass.

ORANGE BLOSSOM

Yield: 1 serving

1 1/2 ounces gin
orange juice

splash of fresh lime juice
splash of simple syrup (sugar syrup)

1. Fill a highball glass with ice. Pour in gin and fill to top with orange juice. Stir in lime juice and simple syrup.

ORANGE BLOSSOM II

Yield: 1 serving

1 1/2 ounces vodka
splash orange liqueur
orange juice
1 ounce champagne

1. Shake the orange liqueur and the vodka in a cocktail shaker filled with ice. Strain into a champagne glass. Carefully pour in champagne so as not to break up bubbles. Float orange juice on top.

ORANGE CRUSH

Yield: 1 serving

1 ounce vodka or orange-flavored vodka
1/2 ounce orange liqueur
4 ounces orange juice

Shake the vodka and the Grand Marnier in a cocktail shaker filled with ice.

Strain and pour into a shooter (tall shot glass). Float orange juice on top.

ORANGE JULIUS

Yield: 1 serving

1 ounce light rum
1 ounce almond liqueur
1/2 ounce orange liqueur
2 ounces orange juice
1 ounce heavy cream
1/2 cup crushed ice

1. Combine all ingredients in a blender. Pour into a tall glass. Garnish with orange slice.

ORANGE MARGARITA

Yield: 1 serving

2 ounces tequila
1 ounce orange liqueur
2 ounces orange juice
1 ounce fresh lime juice
splash of Benedictine™ liqueur, if desired
1/2 cup crushed ice

1. Combine all ingredients in a blender. Pour into a margarita glass rimmed with salt or sugar.

PARADICE ICE

Yield: 1 serving

  1/2 ounce vodka
  1/2 ounce gin
  1/2 ounce coconut rum
  1/2 ounce peach schnapps
  splash of Rose's™ lime juice
  splash of orange juice
  1/2 cup crushed ice

1. Combine all ingredients in a blender. Pour into a hurricane glass. Garnish with orange slice.

PEACH FIZZ

Yield: 1 serving

  2 ounces gin
  1 ounce peach liqueur
  1/2 ounce fresh lemon juice
  1/2 ounce Coco Lopez™
  1 ounce light cream
  club soda

1. Shake all ingredients except club soda in a cocktail shaker filled with ice. Strain into a highball glass. Fill to top with club soda, stirring gently.

PEANUT BUTTER PIE

Yield: 1 serving

  1 ounce Frangelico™
  1 ounce coffee-flavored brandy
  1 ounce brandy
  1 ounce cream

1. Fill a rocks glass with ice. Stir in all ingredients.

PINK PANTHER

Yield: 1 serving

  1 ounce gin
  1/2 ounce dry vermouth
  1/2 ounce Crème de Cassis
  splash of Parfait Amour (violet liqueur)
  1 ounce orange juice

1. Shake all ingredients in a cocktail shaker filled with ice. Strain into a martini glass.

RASPBERRY COCONUT COLADA

Yield: 1 serving

  1 1/2 ounces coconut rum
  1 ounce cherry liqueur

splash of Coco Lopez™
splash of pineapple juice
1/2 cup crushed ice
fresh pineapple slice

1. Combine all ingredients except pineapple slice in a blender. Pour into a hurricane glass. Garnish with pineapple slice.

ROYAL ORANGE BLOSSOM

Yield: 1 serving

1 1/2 ounces gin
1/2 ounce orange liqueur
1/2 ounce almond liqueur
1/2 ounces orange juice

1. Fill a cocktail shaker with ice. Add all ingredients, shake and strain into a martini glass.

RUM RUNNER

Yield: 1 serving

1 ounce 151 proof rum
1 ounce banana liqueur
1/2 ounce Crème de Cassis
splash of almond liqueur

1/2 cup crushed ice
ground nutmeg

1. Combine all ingredients except nutmeg in a blender. Pour into a tall glass. Garnish with nutmeg.

SCARLETT O'HARA

Yield: 1 serving

1 1/2 ounce Southern Comfort™
4 ounces cranberry juice cocktail
splash of fresh lime juice

1. Fill a highball glass with ice. Stir in all ingredients.

SHARK BITE

Yield: 1 serving

1 ounce tequila
1 ounce vodka
splash of hot sauce
lime wedge

1. Splash the hot sauce into the bottom of a shooter. Add tequila and vodka. Squeeze a lime over drink, then drop in.

SLOPPY JOE'S COCKTAIL

Yield: 1 serving

Back in 1851, Captain Tony's Saloon was a morgue and icehouse, then Key West's first telegraph station. From 1933 to 1937 it was Ernest Hemingway's favorite bar, a.k.a. the original Sloppy Joe's. Early in his career, Jimmy Buffet sang here.

  1 ounce light or gold rum
  1/2 ounce dry vermouth
  1/2 ounce Grenadine
  1/2 ounce triple sec
  1 ounce pineapple juice

1. Fill a cocktail shaker with ice. Add drink ingredients, shake and strain into a cocktail glass.

SOUTH OF THE BORDER

Yield: 1 serving

 1 1/2 ounces tequila
 1/2 ounce coffee-flavored brandy
 1/2 ounce fresh lime juice
 lime wedge

1. Fill a low-ball glass with ice. Stir in all ingredients. Squeeze a lime wedge over glass and drop in.

STRAWBERRY DAIQUIRI

Yield: 1 serving

  2 ounces light rum
  1/2 cup frozen strawberries
  splash of Rose's™ lime juice
  1/2 cup crushed ice

1. Blend all ingredients with 1/2 cup ice in blender. Pour into tall glass.

STRAWBERRY DROP

Yield: 1 serving

  1 ounce vodka or strawberry-flavored vodka
  1 ounce strawberry liqueur
  splash of orange liqueur
  splash of cranberry juice cocktail

1. Fill a rocks glass with ice. Stir in all ingredients.

STRAWBERRY MARGARITA

Yield: 1 serving

  2 ounces tequila
  1 ounce strawberry liqueur

1 ounce Triple Sec
2 ounces fresh lime juice
1/2 cup frozen strawberries
1/2 cup crushed ice
1 strawberry

1. Combine all ingredients in a blender except for the one strawberry. Pour into a hurricane glass. Garnish with strawberry.

SWAMPWATER

Yield: 1 serving

1 ounce green Chartreuse™
1 ounce vodka
2 ounces pineapple juice.

1. Fill a rocks glass with ice. Stir in all ingredients.

SWIMMING POOL

Yield: 1 serving

1 ounce vodka
1 ounce light or gold rum
2 ounce pineapple juice
1 ounce Coco Lopez™
splash of Blue Curacao™

1. Combine all ingredients in a blender except for Blue Curacao. Fill a hurricane glass with ice. Pour blender contents into glass. Float Blue Curacao on top.

TOP BANANA

Yield: 1 serving

1 ounce vodka
1 ounce light or gold rum
1 ounce banana liqueur

1. Fill a rocks glass with ice. Stir in all ingredients.

WINDEX

Yield: 1 serving

1 ounce vodka
1 ounce Blue Curacao™
splash of fresh lemon juice

1. Fill a cocktail shaker with ice. Add all ingredients, shake and strain into a shooter glass.

ZOMBIE

Yield: 1 serving

The Madhatter Restaurant existed on the Massachusetts island of Nantucket more than 20 years ago and was known for its potent frozen drink, a Zombie. I was 18 years old when I had my first Zombie. I couldn't finish it, because after a few sips, I couldn't even see.

This has become my signature drink. I don't drink them anymore, but I do put the recipe at the end of nearly all my cookbooks. Each book has a slightly version. Remember, do not drink and drive ever!

    1 ounce light rum
    1 ounce dark rum
    2 ounces pineapple juice
    1 ounce orange juice
    1 ounce fresh lime juice
generous splash of Grenadine syrup
    1 cup crushed ice
1/2 ounce 151 proof rum
pineapple slice

1. Combine all ingredients except pineapple slice and 151-proof rum in a blender until smooth. Float the 151 on top. Garnish with pineapple slice.

BIBLIOGRAPHY

Browning, Jeannine. *Sand in My Shoes*. Melbourne, FL.

Burt, Al. *The Tropic of Cracker (Florida History and Culture Series)*. Florida: University Press of Florida, 1991.

Carlton, Lowis. *Famous Florida Recipes*. St. Petersburg: Great Outdoors Publishing Company.

Carlton, Lowis. *Florida Seafood Cookery*. St. Petersburg: Great Outdoors Publishing Company.

Douglas, Marjorie, Stoneman. *The Everglades: River of Grass*. Sarasota: Pineapple Press, 1997.

Elverson, Virginia. *Gulf Coast Cooking*. Fredericksburg, TX: Shearer Publishing.

Fichter, George, S. *The Sunshine State Cookbook*. Sarasota: Pineapple Press, 2002.

Fischer, Al and Mildred. *Citrus Lover's Cookbook*. Phoenix: Golden West Publishers.

Flagg, William. *Cookin' in the Keys*. Key West: Palm Island Press, 2003.

Florida Strawberry Grower's Association. *Simply Florida...Strawberries*. Plant City, FL: Florida Strawberry Grower's Association.

Fodors LLC. *Fodor's 05 Florida*. New York: Random House, 2005.

Fortin, François, Editorial Director. *The Visual Food Encylopedia*. Montréal: Les Éditions Québec/Amérique, 1996.

Gassenheimer, Linda. *Keys Cuisine*. New York: Atlantic Monthly Press, 1991.

Grand Lagoon Yacht Club. *Good Cooking*. Pensacola: Grand Lagoon Yacht Club.

Harper, Shannon and Cope, Janet. *The Essential Catfish Cookbook*. Sarasota: Pineapple Press.

Junior League of Gainesville. *Gracious Gator Cooks*. Gainsville: Junior League of Gainsville.

Junior Service League of St. Augustine, Inc. *Lighthouse Secrets*. St. Augustine: Junior Service League of St. Augustine.

Junior Service League of Panama City. *Bay Fêtes*. Panama City: Junior Serve League of Panama City.

Mormino, Gary, R. *Land of Sunshine, State of Dreams: A Social History of Modern Florida*. Florida: University of Florida Press, 2005.

Mott, Mrs. Paul, A. *Marion Dragoons Chapter 2311 Cookbook*. Lady Lake, Fl: United Daughters of the Confederacy, Marion Dragoons Chapter #2311.

O'Neal, Catherine. *Hidden Florida: Including Miami, Orlando, Ft. Lauderdale, Tampa Bay, The Everglades, and the Keys*. Berkeley: Ulysses Press, 2003.

Oppel, Frank. *Tales of Old Florida*. Secaucus, NJ: Books Sales, 1991.

Ortiz, Elisabeth Lambert. *The Complete Guide of Caribbean Cooking.* New York: N. Evans and Company, 1967.

Rawlins, Marjorie, Kinnan. *Cross Creek Cookery.* USA: Fireside—Fireside Edition, 1996.

Roberts, Dianne. *Dream State: Eight Generations of Swamp Lawyers, Conquistadors, Confederate Daughters, Banana Republicans, and Other Florida Wildlife.* New York: Free Press, 2004.

The Editors of Cook's Illustrated. *The Best Recipe.* Brookline: Boston Common Press, 1999.

Thurma, Cynthia. *The Mongo Mango Cookbook.* Sarasota: Pineapple Press, Inc.

Voltz, Jeanne, and Stuart, Caroline. *The Florida Cookbook.* New York: Alfred A. Knopf, Inc., 1993.

RESOURCES

Annatto Seed
>Whole Spice   (415)-472-1750   www.wholespice.com

>Bijol and Spices, Inc.

>2154 N.W. 22nd Court
Miami, FL 33142
(305)-634-9030   bijol@earthlink.net

Citrus, luscious oranges and grapefruits sent to your door
>FloridaOrange.com

Datil Dew Pepper Sauces and Pickles
>Datil Dew Products
St. Augustine, FL
(904)-284-8144   www.pepperproducts.com

Tupelo honey: Orange Blossom, Tupelo, Palmetto, Unfiltered Tropical Wild Tupelo honey, Citrus Tupelo honey with Key Lime or Tangerine
>Tropical Blossom Tupelo Honey Co., Inc.
106 North Ridgewood Ave.
Edgewater, Fl 32132
(386)-428-9027
(386)-423-8469   www.tropicbeeTupelohoney.com

Key Lime Juice
>Florida Key West, Inc.
5470 Division Drive
Ft. Meyers, FL 33905
(239)-694-8787
www.florida-juice.com

Key Lime Products: Candy, Pies, Jellies, Marmalades, Sauces, Dips, Bath & Body
>Key Lime Products
Key Largo, FL
(800)-870-1780   www.keylimeproducts.com

GLOSSARY OF INGREDIENTS AND TERMS

Aji Dulce: (*Capsicum annuum*) Sweet chili pepper, a dwarf with a mild and distinct flavor. Not to be confused with hot peppers.

Annatto: (*Achiote*) The use of *achiote* to flavor and color food has always been an important part of traditional island food. When combined with other herbs and spices, this emulsion gives Cuban and Puerto Rican cuisine its distinctive aroma and flavor. Annatto dates back to the Tainos who called it *bixa*.

Lard or vegetable oil is heated in a saucepan at *low* heat, together with *achiote* seeds to release a rich, orange-yellow color and mildly pungent flavor. The seeds are then strained and the emulsion reserved in a jar.

Annatto's uses vary from flavoring and coloring rice dishes, adding an orange-brown color to white meats, substituting for tomatoes, to adding complexity to vegetable dishes. The use of this flavoring and coloring agent was the most efficient way to deal with the many staples not found in the kitchens of Spanish colonial Puerto Rico. Known as the poor man's saffron.

Bijol: Poor man's substitute for saffron. Yellow in color, it is made from ground annatto seed, occasionally with a touch of oregano, cumin and other spices.

Boniata: Also known as a white sweet potato.

Breadfruit: (*pana, panapen*) Large, roundish fruit (some as large as a soccer ball) of a tropical tree. A thick, greenish rind covers the sweet, starch flesh similar in taste to a potato. Do not eat raw. Fried green bread fruit are served as *tostones* to accompany drinks, meats, chicken or fish.

Calamondin: Cross between a kumquat and a tangerine. Fruit is sour, often substituted for lemons or limes, makes a wonderful marmalade. Looks like a tiny orange.

Cactus Pear: Also known as a prickly pear, an edible cactus found in tropical regions. Fruit is deep red, used in salads.

Carambola: Also called a starfruit, yellow, with shiny, waxlike skin, sliced crosswise, it resembles a star. Use in salads, or as a side dish to fish, poultry or meat. Sweet to acid in flavor. Juice makes a refreshing drink. Can be used in preserves that have a tart, quincelike flavor.

Cassava: Tuber of a shrub that has large palmate leaves. Can grow up to ten feet in height, native to Brazil and Mexico. Also known as manioc, not to be confused with yucca. Tuber is conical in shape, brown skinned, and the flesh can be white, yellow or red. Tubers can grow up to three feet in length and weigh 50 pounds or more. There are many varieties of cassava, all of which contain hydrocyanic acid, a poisonous substance eliminated by cooking or dehydration. Used to make tapioca.

Chayote: (Christophene) Pear-shaped, looks like a pale avocado, grows on a climbing plant extensively in the Caribbean and Florida. Similar in flavor to summer squash.

Chile Pepper: Both the scotch bonnet and Datil pepper grow freely in Florida. Scotch bonnets are popular with Caribbean transplants and Floridians alike. Datil peppers were grown originally by the Minorcans in St. Augustine. Both peppers are fiery hot, so use with care.

Chorizo: Highly seasoned Spanish pork sausage, sun-dried and hot to palate.

Cilantro: Coriander leaves

Coconut: (*Coco*) The use of coconut in Hispanic households is divided into two categories: *fresco de agua* (ripe with water) and *seco* (dry). The ripe with water coconuts are used in the making of desserts. The water is drained and used for making rum drinks, or simply as a reviving, non-alcoholic beverage. The dry coconut is used to make coconut milk and intensely flavored sauces.

Condensed Milk: Not to be confused with evaporated milk. Sweetened condensed milk is a blend of whole milk and sugar, with 60 percent of its water removed, and is very important to Key Lime Pie. Thickens naturally in the presence of an acid, such as Key Lime juice. Tinned, and unopened, it keeps for a long time.

Culantro: (*recao*)

Long, serrated leaves of a small herb, wide coriander leaf, which grows wild in the Caribbean and Florida.

Evaporated milk: Whole milk that has been cooked to reduce its water content by 60%. Evaporated skim milk contains 0.5 percent butterfat. Do not mix up with sweetened condensed milk. The two are not interchangeable.

Flan: Custard

Gandul or gandules: Green pigeon peas

Ginger: (*Fengibre*) A spicy root, ginger is the main ingredient in Island Bouquet Garni. Ginger is best when fresh. Purchase only as much as you will immediately need.

Green Onions: (*Cebollin*) Also known as scallions, used for their subtle flavor enhancement in sauces, salads, meat, fish and poultry. The high water content of scallions is beneficial when sautéing herbs as it will provide some liquid to the drier ingredients. Garlic will cook and burn quickly upon a hot surface, but scallions will slow down the reaction time. Another use is to absorb some of the strong odors given off by lamb or seafood during cooking.

Guava: Native to tropical America, this fruit is rich in vitamin C. High in pectin; it can be easily be cooked into a paste. Intense, perfumy flavor. Skin is green to pale yellow, with flesh color ranging from cream to strawberry red.

Ham: (*Jamon*) Smoked cured ham is indispensable in the Latin kitchen. Used as a base for *sofrito,* and for soups, rice, main courses, etc.

Ham is used for pork fillings in *pastels, alcapurria* and *empanadas.*

Italian seasoning: Dried rosemary, oregano, basil, thyme, etc. May be purchased in the bottled herb section of the grocer.

Key Limes: *Citrus aurantifolio* grows to about fifteen feet, and may have originated with the sour orange tree from the East Indies. Key limes are yellow, not green, which means Key Lime pies are also yellow.

Kumquat: Resembles a miniature orange, may be eaten whole, seeds, skin and all. Used in fish dishes and marmalades.

Loquats: Native to China, grows in tropics year round. Yellowish-orange, pear-shaped fruit made into preserves or jelly.

Olive Oil: (*Aceite de Oliva*) Centuries ago, olive oil was highly prized in the New World, not just for cooking, but as a lamp oil, and lubricant for machinery. Because of piracy and foul weather, often it would be one or two years before a cargo ship reached Florida and the Keys. Prices on commodities and necessities soared, including olive oil.

Pigeon Peas: A type of legume about the size of peas. Can be purchased canned.

Plantain: (*Amarillo*) Fruit of the banana tree, a giant herbaceous plant native to Malaysia, related to the sweet banana. Also known as the 'cooking banana.' Ten to fifteen inches long, its green skin is thicker than that of the banana, its flesh firmer and not as sweet. When fully ripe, the skin turns black. Not to be eaten raw.

Recaíto: Seasoning made with recao, cilantro, onion, garlic and peppers that adds a distinctive flavor to food. Always part of the *sofrito* base.

Sofrito: Base for Latin cooking made from *recaíto* cooked with ham, tomato sauce and/or *achiote* (annatto).

Swamp Cabbage: a.k.a. hearts of palm. Difficult to find fresh, the core center of young palms can be found canned at the grocer. Serve in salad or as a vegetable.

Yautía: Starchy root (taro) of a tropical, large-leaved plant. Flesh is creamy white or yellow, similar in flavor and texture to Irish or Idaho potato.

Yuca: See cassava.

INDEX

Bold page numbers indicate drinks.

Indexed by:
Clive Pyne Book Indexing Services

A NOTE ABOUT THE AUTHOR

ANGELA SPENCELEY was born in Stoughton, Massachusetts. Twenty-five years ago she moved to St. Thomas in the U.S. Virgin Islands, where she is the editor and chief writer for a Caribbean publishing firm, Coconut Press, LLC.

She has authored eleven cookbooks, including: *A Taste of the Caribbean; A Taste of the Virgin Islands; A Taste of Puerto Rico; A Taste of Puerto Rico, Too!; Just Add Rum!; Don't Drink the Water—The Complete Caribbean Bartending Guide; My Tiny Virgin Island Cookbook; How to Have Your Own Caribbean Luau; and A Taste of Florida, The Keys and Caribbean, A Taste of the British Virgin Islands and A Taste of St. Croix..* She has also written two guidebooks: *Walking Tour Guide to St. Thomas, U.S. Virgin Islands and Guide to the U.S. Virgin Islands (Revised).*

Ms. Spenceley divides her time between St. Thomas, Puerto Rico and Miami, where she is a food consultant, writer and publisher.

PLEASE SEND ME THE FOLLOWING

QUAN.	ITEM			PRICE
_____	A Taste of Florida and The Keys	approx. 180pp	($14.99)	_____
_____	A Taste of the Caribbean Cookbook			
	Over 250 traditional and novelle recipes	approx. 292pp	($19.99)	_____
_____	A Taste of the Virgin Islands Cookbook	approx. 032pp	($9.99)	_____
_____	A Taste of Puerto Rico Cookbook	approx. 032pp	($8.99)	_____
_____	A Taste of Puerto Rico, Too! Cookbook	approx. 400pp	($19.99)	_____
_____	A Taste of the British Virgin Islands Cookbook	approx. 060pp	($9.99)	_____
_____	A Taste of St. Croix Cookbook	approx. 060pp	($9.99)	_____
_____	Don't Drink the Water, *Complete Caribbean Bartending Guide*		($19.99)	_____
_____	Just Add Rum! Cookbook and drink guide	approx. 120pp	($9.99)	_____
_____	How to Have Your Own Caribbean Luau	approx. 096pp	($9.99)	_____
_____	My Tiny Virgin Island Cookbook	approx. 042pp	($5.99)	_____

OTHER CARIBBEAN BOOKS

_____	**Guide to the U.S. Virgin Islands**		
	English or Spanish, approx. 96pp of Color Photos	($18.99)	_____
_____	**Guide to Puerto Rico**		
	English or Spanish, approx. 96pp of Color Photos	($18.99)	_____
_____	**Guide to the British Virgin Islands**		
	English or Spanish, approx. 96pp of Color Photos	($18.99)	_____
_____	**Flowers of the Caribbean,** *64 stunning pages*	($14.99)	_____

SHIPPING

Continental U.S. *Add $5.00 for first item, and $3.00 per additional item sent to same address.*
International & Canada *Add $15.00 for first item, and $10.00 per additional item sent to same address.*

SUBTOTAL _____
SALES TAX _____
SHIPPING _____
TOTAL _____

NAME _____

ADDRESS _____

CITY _____ STATE _____ ZIP _____

TELEPHONE _____ FAX _____ EMAIL _____

PAYMENT

■ Checks payable to: **Coconut Press, LLC**
   Mail to: PO Box 79710, Carolina, PR 00984-9710

■ **Secure Fax orders:** (787) 253-8449. Fill out this form & fax.

■ **Contact:** Angelaspenceley1@msn.com I www.coconut-press.com